INTO PROFIT
Turning your company round for dramatic results

INTO PROFIT

Turning your company
round for dramatic results

Bill Scott

McGRAW-HILL BOOK COMPANY

London · New York · St Louis · San Francisco · Auckland · Bogotá
Caracas · Hamburg · Lisbon · Madrid · Mexico · Milan · Montreal
New Delhi · Panama · Paris · San Juan · São Paulo · Singapore
Sydney · Tokyo · Toronto

Published by
McGRAW-HILL Book Company (UK) Limited
SHOPPENHANGERS ROAD · MAIDENHEAD · BERKSHIRE
ENGLAND
Telephone: 0628-23432 FAX: 0628-770224

British Library Cataloguing in Publication Data

Scott, Bill
  Into profit : turning your company round for dramatic
  results.
  1. Business firms. Profitability
  I. Title
  338.7

  ISBN 0-07-707453-X

Library of Congress Cataloging-in-Publication Data

Scott, Bill
    Into profit : turning your company round for dramatic results /
  Bill Scott.
      p.   cm.
    Includes index.
    ISBN 0-07-707453-X
    1. Corporate turnarounds—Management.   I. Title.
  HD58.8.S388   1991
  658.1′6—dc20   90-20162
                                                          CIP

1 2 3 4 5 CUP   954321

Typeset by Rowland Phototypesetting Limited
Bury St Edmunds, Suffolk
and printed and bound in Great Britain
at the University Press, Cambridge

Contents

Preface

THE PROBLEM FACING YOU

This book is written for the general manager, chief executive or managing director who is attempting a business turn round. In plain language that implies your company is making losses and that your own personal survival, just as much as the survival of your company, depends on getting out of the red and back at least to a break-even point within a reasonably short time-scale.

For the time being, at any rate, objectives of earnings per share, return on capital employed or any other yardstick of a successful business are overshadowed by the much more stark and elementary arithmetic of turning a minus figure into a plus figure.

You need help, and that is what this book is meant to give. I stress help because there are no instant remedies. I have been there myself. I could have used help and so often did not find it. This book sums up all that I have had to learn the hard way.

This is not an exhaustive textbook on business management methods. It will concentrate on sound practical advice rather than pure theory. You can get all the theory you need by visiting a good business library.

In my own career I have turned three companies round from a loss-making position, so I realize full well, just as you yourself do, what it is like to work in problem companies. I have done so for over ten years.

I know how lonely it can be taking all the responsibility with no shoulder to cry on. How hard it can be to slog along for so long, believing that you are on the right road, but with the signs of progress coming always too slowly. And I know what it feels like both to succeed and to fail. There is a very narrow dividing line between success and failure, and, just as important, initial success is a very fragile thing indeed, like a flower bud exposed to a late frost.

YOUR OWN POSITION

What I do not know is what business you are in, but that is not too important because the advice I have will apply equally to manufacturing or to distribution, and a large part of it will also be relevant to service industries.

I also do not know whether you own your own company or whether you are an employee, and, in the latter case, whether or not your company is part of a larger group. These are important factors when we later come to work out what action to take.

Yet again, I do not know if your problem is that of a new company which has not yet fully taken off. New business ventures, like nuclear reactions, need to reach a certain critical mass before taking off. This book is much more concerned with turning round established businesses that have gone wrong somewhere along the way.

What I do know is that you have a turn-round problem on your hands. What is more, you may well have only recently inherited this problem; in fact, this book assumes that this is so. If you have been in the hot seat for some time, you may well already be some way along the path that this book suggests. Nevertheless you may still find some new ideas here.

I would guess that your business is relatively small, say with a turnover of less than £5 million a year, and probably closer to £1 million. Once you get bigger, and certainly by the time your turnover is over £20 million a year, the cost of employing high-powered consultants or 'company doctors' to solve the problem becomes of less significance in terms of short-term costs, and you might well already have more help to hand than I can possibly offer in this book.

One thing is certain—it is that your job is just about the most difficult one you could have wished for:

- You have a big problem on your hands.
- But you have very limited means at your disposal.

Your job is in many respects more difficult than that of the chairman of a large multinational corporation; however big that problem may be, the multinational chairman is not likely to be as short of the people and money resources needed to tackle the problem as you are.

SOME PERSONAL ADVICE FOR YOU

At this stage, until we get to more concrete matters, I can give you only some immediate and personal advice. Your own attitude to the task you face will be of great importance and among the key factors for success will be these:

- Determination to succeed
- A vision of where you are headed
- Not relying on luck
- Making the experience an enjoyable one

Determination

You are going to need a lot of grit and determination, if you are to succeed. Kipling is not a very fashionable source of inspiration today, but I do counsel you to take to heart what he said about facing triumph and disaster: 'and treat these two imposters just the same'. In your situation the dividing line between them is often very narrow indeed.

About watching the 'things you gave your life to broken, and stoop and build them up again with worn out tools': you may have to do this more than once and it may be a long time before you can afford the luxury of tools that are not worn out. Lastly, take heed of what Kipling said of the 'unforgiving minute', because you will need every 60 seconds' worth in the days and months ahead.

The Importance of Vision

You are also going to need a vision of where you are headed. I was once given the advice that a strategic plan was no substitute for a vision of where to go next. Sometimes it helps to look to others for a successful model to follow. Let me give you an example.

Frank Perkins founded the Perkins Engine Company just after the Second World War. He started from very humble origins in a back street in Peterborough, and in time his business grew to become the world's leading manufacturer of diesel engines. I worked for this company for a few years in the late sixties, and I still remember Frank Perkins' motto, which was engraved above the main entrance to the office block where I worked: 'Where there is no vision the people perish.' That comes from the Book of Proverbs and is just about the most relevant single bit of advice you can be given.

The Element of Luck

It will be a very big help to you if you have luck on your side, but you certainly cannot count on it. Many sales managers believe that what they need most of all is not so much a good sales team as a lucky sales team. But is that element of so-called luck really understood?

The lucky salesperson is the one who walks through the right door at the right time. But is that really luck? Or is it just that good salespeople are more perceptive, ask the right questions and hear the answers, and so are able to sense or judge exactly when to walk through that door?

The lucky manager is the one who finds the big opportunity at the right time. It usually comes to those who have the time to go out looking for opportunities, but you are going to spend so much time with your nose to the grindstone that you will not be in this fortunate position for some time to come.

It Must Be Enjoyable

Whether luck smiles on you or passes you by on the other side is something you cannot influence. There is one thing you can influence though, and it is very important. The job of turning this company round must be something you can enjoy. Not only that, you must make it enjoyable for everyone else in the company. You will succeed faster if everyone has a bit of fun from time to time.

1

Managing people and seeking help

This book will give you a methodology that will enable you to turn your company round from loss to profit. It addresses the vital steps of fact-finding, analysis and planning, and a very great deal of that is a thinking process. The most important step of all, however, is that of putting your plans into action and achieving the end-results. To succeed in that you must be expert in managing and motivating the people who work at all levels in your company. In turn you will need a large amount of help from them and from many other sources as well.

In this first chapter we shall therefore take time to consider two of the most important ingredients in the overall formula for success:

- Managing people in a turn-round situation
- Identifying sources of help

MANAGING PEOPLE

The size of business you are managing is probably too small to justify a separate personnel function. That means that you have to be your own personnel manager. If your experience in this field is limited, you would be well advised at the outset to turn for help to a good textbook on personnel management.

For the most part the art of managing people in your special situation is not dramatically different from what would be good practice in a healthy business. All you have learned or been taught on this subject will be both relevant and necessary here and now. You must, however, address a number of problems that you would not expect to find in a healthy company:

- The problem is time-critical.
- There is an urgency about achieving results.
- Employee morale may already be low.
- It is more difficult to offer incentives or rewards.
- Your leadership will be the key factor.
- You must resolve differing attitudes to the loss-making position.

In a loss-making position you have a finite amount of time in which to produce results. Just how much time you have is a matter we shall examine in more detail in Chapter 5, but it does not alter the fact that you must accept and respond to the urgency of achieving results.

A key factor in doing so is going to be the way in which you motivate and manage the people at all levels in this business. On the shopfloor, in the offices and above all within your management team, you are going to find that you will need above-average improvements in performance within a shorter than usual time-scale in order to reverse the decline that has taken place over the past. In other words, you are going to have to be better at managing and motivating people than most managers of healthy companies need to be.

The problem is that you will almost certainly start with a number of major disadvantages which will make that task even more difficult. If the company has been making a loss for some time, and especially if it has been poorly managed over that period, you may find that morale throughout the company is at a low ebb and still sinking fast, despite your own arrival on the scene. That is going to make it so much more difficult to nudge performance upwards. A little bit of success may begin to cure that quite easily, but you may not be able to guarantee that in the very immediate future.

The Effect of Pay Freezes

Your business will be short of money. This means you will most probably have to consider a pay freeze as well as a freeze on further recruitment. You may also have to suspend overtime working, and that will actually reduce the take-home pay of most of your employees. These measures will have a demotivating effect, especially if the rate of inflation is relatively high. What is important is that you counter this by undertaking to review the situation in three or six months' time, when the company may well have started to earn profits again.

Time-scales are important. You can make it clear that your employees will share in the success when it takes place and not have to sit it out until the next annual pay review falls due. When you do come to review pay make sure you have an eye on local market pay levels. Keeping your company rates of pay in line with the local market will be a surer way of keeping or attracting good staff than dealing in arbitrary percentage awards.

The Difficulty of Offering Incentives

It is much more difficult in a loss-making position to offer the monetary rewards or incentives that can act as the 'carrot' to improvements in performance. You simply do not have the money available.

Many of the common means of offering monetary incentives have drawbacks in a loss-making position:

- Incentives related to productivity improvements may actually make your bottom-line results worse unless you have a growing sales order book and need additional capacity, or unless you cash in on the productivity improvements by reducing the head-count.
- Profit-related incentives may take too many months into the future before they translate into hard cash in people's pockets.
- Rewards based on bottom-line improvement: if you were to share with your employees an affordable part of any

improvement in the bottom-line results over the coming months, it may not add up to very much in terms of a tangible reward.

There is a number of things you can consider:

- Performance-related awards: by setting targets or operating a simple appraisal system. With these you should be aiming to foster teamwork and not individualism.
- Review the overall pay/benefit/working conditions package: you may not be able to do much about the pay element, but there may be other elements that can be enhanced at comparatively little cost to the company; these may have a relatively high perceived benefit. One example is life assurance cover for employees, where a group scheme can provide cover for a fraction of what it would cost employees if they negotiated individually.

The Importance of Your Leadership

The most important factor in countering these problems and re-motivating your staff is going to be you yourself. It is going to hinge on your leadership and on the example you set to everyone in the company.

The key to providing leadership in this situation lies in a number of very basic points:

- Help people to believe in success.
- Identify closely with them.
- Be visible and keep smiling.
- Establish your own credibility.

You must believe that you are going to succeed and you must make the people in the company believe that with your leadership you will achieve success together. Unless it is your natural style, avoid the 'action man' role. Resist, for example, the temptation to fire some managers simply to prove that you are not afraid to take drastic action. You may very well need to prune the dead wood out of your management team, but do it at the right time and for the right reasons. Avoid also the politician's gimmicks, like a programme for 'the first 100 days'; your critical time-scale may in real life be shorter, or longer, than that.

One key to getting your people to respond will be how well and how closely you identify with them. It is very tempting when you are new and inherit problems to talk of these to your people as if the problems were theirs or your predecessor's. The day you took on this job they became your own problems, and it will help you to identify with your staff if you describe these as 'our problems'. Emphasize the 'we', 'us' and 'our'. It implies that you are with your people and not against them. That may be refreshing, reassuring and a welcome change from the past.

It is also important that you are seen as often as possible on the shopfloor and around the offices, and that you keep smiling. When you spend all your days locked away in your own office, or when you appear in the factory with worry showing on your face, people will assume the worst.

Establish Your Credibility

Above all you must quickly establish your personal credibility. The key to this is very simple:

- Be seen to make good decisions.
- Make decisions quickly.
- Produce ideas and initiatives that are seen to work.
- Encourage others to offer their own ideas.

The worst style of leadership is the one that assumes that the people on the shopfloor have nothing to contribute except working harder. Even today it is not uncommon. It is surprising just how perceptive people in non-thinking jobs can be when it comes to discerning whether or not the company is being led in the right direction. It is also discussed very frequently.

The decisions you make will be judged by people at all levels in the company. They may not all have the degree of intelligence you possess, but they will none the less very soon sort out the good decisions from the bad. The end-result after all usually speaks for itself. The ability to make decisions that are seen to be good, and to make them quickly, is a vital factor in determining how your people will respond to you.

Just as important is what you yourself are seen to contribute in terms of ideas for improvements and the initiatives that are seen to originate from your own office. This is where it helps if you have hands-on experience in some aspects of the business or have good advice readily available to you. Equally, the willingness with which you encourage and promote the good ideas of others in the company will in the end yield you the same degree of credibility.

Attitudes to the Loss-making Situation

The biggest mistake you could possibly make would be to expect people to deliver the extra performance you need *just because* the company is loss-making. That is rarely a motivating factor, except in the odd case of very long-serving employees who genuinely see the larger part of their life's work invested in the company. Recognizing these people, if they exist, and using them as a communications bridge to others can often be a very powerful force.

Personal attitudes to the loss-making position will vary considerably. How you respond and begin to re-motivate is a matter where you should distinguish between your management team and the rest of the workforce.

The Management Team

With your immediate management team you certainly need to foster an acute appreciation of the 'crisis' you face together. For the right managers this could represent a real challenge, just as it presumably does for you. The shared success in turning this company round ought to be a powerful motivation in itself, especially as this will enhance their future career prospects.

But whether this works or not yet again depends almost entirely on your own leadership. It depends on you making them believe that you have both the ability and the determination to succeed, and it will be helped by the vision you offer them of the future to which you are leading them and the company.

In a loss-making situation you have a greater need than ever to achieve unity of purpose within that management team. That unity will stem largely from the ease with which the team can establish a consensus of views. If you need to argue the toss with any manager over a policy, do it in private and then try to present an agreed solution to your colleagues. That way you will make it as easy as possible for the team to unite. Again, the unity of the management team is something that has a habit of being highly visible to a great many people in the company. They will be more easily motivated when they see their leaders are united.

Prune out the Dead Wood

If you have dead wood in your management team, you must act quickly. You should be in a position to identify the dead wood within your first month. The longer you leave problems like this unattended, the more they become seen as *your* problems, rather than the problems inherited from your predecessor.

You should insist on making provisions for termination payments in the previous month's accounts, or better still in the previous year's accounts, if these have not yet been finalized. At this stage err on the generous side and make provision for one year's salary plus benefits in kind. It may not cost that much and, if you are lucky, you may have change left over at the end of the day that you can release for more constructive purposes without anyone being the wiser. You should find little difficulty in persuading your auditors to agree to this.

Taking this step at an early stage has the great advantage that it then allows you to solve the problem of the dead wood in your own way and at the right time, but without having to face the unwelcome financial impact in a future month's accounts.

The Shopfloor

When it comes to the people on the shopfloor and in the offices, the attitude to a loss-making position is almost as varied as human nature itself. There are some to whom it could represent a challenge if led from the front, just as it should to you and your management team. But to many more it will trigger feelings of insecurity and worry, which rarely contribute to higher performance.

What you should avoid is using the loss-making position as the 'stick' for exacting improved performance. It never works, nor should it. You can do no harm by explaining the blunt facts, especially to supervisors or to a works committee, so that no one is under any misunderstanding about the company's real position, but you must be prepared for the response that they see that as your problem. And, of course, they are quite right. If you are new to the job, you may find that when you do set out the position clearly, the reaction is: 'We have heard it all before'. That attitude will change only when *you* deliver something for the better.

The Customer Pays the Wages

There is an alternative approach you can take which will produce results very much more easily. It is to preach the message that it is the customers who pay the wages. The elementary truth of this is never difficult to convey, provided you present it carefully. Most people take a great deal of pride in the work they do. Once they associate the customers' satisfaction with their continuing weekly wages, the thought that they might let down a customer will offend their sense of pride. Attitudes to delivery performance and quality, for example, can change very quickly as a result.

You should not see this as a subterfuge tactic; the customer ultimately *does* pay the wages, including your own. If you really believe it, you can use this to motivate people towards improvements in performance in a way that the 'stick' of on-going losses can never do.

The key to making it work effectively is to let the customers tell your people how much better the product quality or service has become. When you are able to take customers round your factory and let them tell your people that they are impressed with the improvements of recent weeks or months, then you will have homed in on a very powerful motivator indeed.

In much the same way, if you are getting the act together, then many things in this company will begin to improve very quickly. When that happens, make it known. Let everyone know how important a part they have played and let it be known that you appreciate it to the full, even if the financial results do not yet justify a reward in money terms.

The Messages You Convey

Part of the art of personnel management is how you communicate with people at all levels. In a loss-making business a great deal will hinge on the messages you convey to your staff. We can sum up this review of managing people by listing the most important messages you have to convey to them:

- You can and will succeed.
- You have a clear vision of the future.
- High performance is needed, and quickly.
- Customer satisfaction is all-important.
- You will provide the leadership.
- Success depends on good teamwork.
- Everyone will share the rewards of success.

WHERE TO SEEK HELP

In addition to being a good manager of people, you must at the outset recognize that you will need a very great deal of help in the task you have taken on. From time to time you are going to read in the business pages how a relatively young and inexperienced high-flying manager of a public group turned a subsidiary company round from loss to profit in a few months. You may perhaps feel some sense of inadequacy that you cannot match that achievement.

The truth of the matter is that the well-publicized turn rounds often owe their success to the fact that a cash-rich parent group spent upwards of £1000 per man-day employing a team of well-known consultants for weeks on end to do the hard nitty-gritty analytical and planning work that you may end up doing single-handed.

The manager of the business unit you read about most probably had access to highly professional accountants, engineers, personnel and marketing people from within the group head office to support the turn round, and even do a large part of the real work, while the manager orchestrated a bought-in rescue plan. If you had that sort of help, you would already be within sight of the winning post.

Where, then, can you turn to for help? The sources of help you should consider are these:

- Your parent group
- Your own management team
- The layers below management level
- New blood
- An unbiased sounding board
- External consultants

Your Parent Group

If your company is part of a larger group, you have a right to expect help from them; but just how much help will be available could depend on the type of group of which you are a part. A recent article distinguished between 'left-handed' groups and 'right-handed groups'. One is marketing-biased, the other is financially-biased.

The latter is hard-nosed, interested only in the numbers and is usually controlled from a relatively small head office. The only real expertise within the group head office is likely to be in financial accounting. There will probably be no marketing or technical help that you can call on, nor any in-group R & D that could contribute to the development of new products. What will be worse is if the subsidiary you are managing is disqualified from any government assistance because it is part of a group with over 2500 employees.

Groups that are marketing-biased are more likely to be vertically integrated. You may well find that items like staff training and PR are centrally funded, and there may well be budgets that can be called on to provide real help in your task of turning this subsidiary round to profit. That can make an enormous difference.

If you are part of a larger group, and especially if you are new in the job, shout from the rooftops for the help you need and make sure the bill stays in head office. Ask all the staff managers whether they have a budget that can help you tackle your problem; and if they do not, try persuading them to ask for a budget so they can help you, because in many groups these staff may have more clout than you have.

Your Management Team

The most obvious place to seek help is clearly within the company. Nothing, but nothing, will be a more certain recipe for success than a strong management team working towards the common goal of success, but the chances are that yours is lacking in many vital respects, otherwise the business would not be in its present position. That limits you, but you must at least begin to sort out the wheat from the chaff.

What talent is there waiting in the wings to be promoted? Good managers rarely recruit low-calibre subordinates, but there are many poor managers with a wealth of talent below them which they have never recognized. Not everyone is fired with the ambition to become a high-powered manager, scanning the recruitment pages weekly for their next move. It does not follow that such people cannot do a sterling job given some coaching and the right encouragement.

Look Below the Management Layer

If you are lucky, you will find a couple of managers whom you will be able to cast in roles that will turn out to be a great strength to you, not only as managers, but as sources of help in solving the fundamental problems you face. But where else can you look for this type of help? Before you go outside the company, look a little deeper below the surface. Your management team may leave a lot to be desired, but what about your shopfloor supervisors and the people you have in staff or administrative jobs?

Get to know the supervisors. And the shopfloor operators. Listen to anyone who talks sense. You may find a lot more knowledge and potential help than you first imagined. The answers to many of the problems facing you may already exist within that pool of talent, but may have been prevented from surfacing by the management styles of the past. Unlocking that may be one of your most powerful sources of help.

Should any of your managers object to this type of participation, simply ask them to write down on a sheet of paper when they last asked their supervisors for advice on a company problem and what action was taken. If you find them staring at a blank sheet, you may have identified the dead wood more clearly.

Looking for New Blood

An injection of new blood into a problem company is always good. Fresh minds will see opportunities for improvement rather than long-standing, intractable problems. At the same time, you have to recognize that a company with big problems like yours is not the most attractive potential employer. The bright, young, potential managers looking for the next rung up on the ladder will usually have options open to them that involve much less of a down-side risk than joining you. And you are almost certainly not in a position immediately to offer premium salaries to attract the right calibre of management. External recruitment is also that much more difficult if you are based in an area of relatively low unemployment like the south-east.

Despite those drawbacks there will always be opportunities for you to find someone capable of doing the job. Consider the following, for example:

- Closure or cut-back by a major local company
- The pool of redundant executives
- Executive leasing

From time to time a major group may cut back quite severely; that may have a spin-off effect on the fortunes of quite a few local subcontractors. For a while there can be a wealth of talent available even in an area of low unemployment. Look under every stone and ask all the local employment agencies who they have on their registers, but without giving them a brief committing you to payment unless the right person turns up.

There is also a large number of discarded executives who are disqualified by age for most of the attractive jobs on offer. A recent survey found that 95 per cent of the job advertisements at executive level specified an upper age limit of 45 years. Many people over this age still have a great deal of energy and creative talent, and a surprising number of them are sufficiently flexible to learn new ways, but you have to be very much more discerning in your interview techniques in order to select wisely. Provided you do choose prudently, the length and breadth of their work experience can far outweigh the negative aspect of their age.

Executive leasing is another option you could consider. The cost will be higher than having someone on the payroll, but you have little or no downside risk if the arrangements do not work out to your satisfaction. You could regard this as a short-term expedient until the company is nursed back to profit, after which you should once again become an attractive employer.

Find a Sounding Board
A very important source of help to you is going to be the shoulder to cry on, or the sounding board you can bounce ideas off and get a

pure and unbiased reaction, with no axes to grind. A sort of father confessor. There will be too many axes grinding within the company by this time if you are going about things the right way, so you need someone outside the company to play this role for you.

If you are part of a group, you should find this support somewhere within the group. After all, what is a boss for? Not to mention all the attendant staff in the corridors of power. But it does not always work that way. Your problem-child company will also be a very big problem from the group's point of view. You would be wise, in terms of your personal position, to be very open and frank in discussing the company problems and in communicating information to group. But if you find group political undercurrents obscuring or confusing the help and advice you need, it is time to seek a sounding board well away from head office.

In one company I managed one of my former bosses became my sounding board. He had lived through exactly the same problems that I was then facing and was able to relate his experience to my own problems. In another company a similar role was played by one of my overseas sales agents. He was far enough removed to be objective, but he understood my business and, because he had a longer association with the company than I did, also knew our people and the history and mistakes of the past.

It will pay you to find someone like that. This will be the person who can listen to your problems and offer advice. Without causing offence, this person will able both to suggest the downside risks in some of your plans and to offer you possible alternatives.

Management Consultants

There are sound arguments for using management consultants to help you in the task of turning your company round and there are also some drawbacks you must be aware of.

You will be in a better position to judge for yourself whether or not you need consultancy help once you have read this book, particularly the latter half, which will guide you to a strategy for recovery. This process will require a very great deal of fact-finding and analysis and also a very special type of thinking process. The advantages of using consultants to do that work, or to help with it, are these:

- It relieves pressure on your own time.
- It brings specialized knowledge and experience.
- It introduces objectivity.

You and your management team have a business to run on a day-to-day basis as well as planning for its recovery. The work-load involved in tackling all of the fact-finding and analysis may be greater than you can sensibly devote to it, and if you curtail that work to fit the time available, you will be very unlikely to arrive at the right answers.

Much of this work will be done more quickly and more thoroughly by people who have either the specialist skills or who have had previous experience of doing it.

The planning process requires a great deal of objective thinking. At some point it will be essential to expose this to an unbiased outsider. Even if you have found someone to be your sounding board, you may be stretching the bonds of friendship too far to expect help in the depth that will be needed.

The drawbacks you must weigh up are these:

- The cost
- The difficulty of finding the right consultant

A consultancy project of this type will cost a great deal of money, probably substantially more than any other item of expenditure you currently have in your budget. The cost of this may be reduced if you qualify for assistance through the Enterprise Initiative programme, but the amount of subsidized consultancy available to you may not be sufficient to do the job as thoroughly and as professionally as it needs to be.

The present market in management consultancy is like a

minefield for the inexperienced seeker of consultancy help, mainly
as a result of the vast proliferation of practices that have emerged
in order to satisfy a rapidly growing market. Many of the so-called
consultants who may approach you are in reality no more than
self-employed salespeople. Choosing the right consultant for this
job is critical to your own success. Selecting the wrong one will not
only cost you money you cannot afford, but may not help you
bring about your turn round.

The very well-known names in the business will almost certainly lead you along the road to success, provided you implement
their recommendations professionally, but their costs will be as
high as their reputation. That may lead you to consider less
well-known firms and so into an area of higher risk of making the
wrong choice.

You should seek help from your auditors or your bank manager
in choosing consultants, or alternatively make your choice based
on the personal recommendation of someone you know and trust,
and who has had a similar assignment carried out satisfactorily.
Appendix 2 (page 240) contains a short check-list of questions to
help you avoid making the wrong choice.

If you are part of a larger group, you should be making a strong
case at the very outset to have the group engage one or other of the
best-known specialists in the business to help you right away;
with the bills being picked up at group level.

Get a Personal Computer and a Spreadsheet

Before leaving the subject of help we have to think of one more
item. You will need a personal computer (PC) and a spreadsheet.
You are going to have to do a great deal of 'number-crunching' in
the weeks and months ahead. There are good buys and bad buys
in the PC field, and there is a considerable choice of spreadsheet
packages available, but this book is not about hardware and
software selection.

If you are not already equipped, then ask advice from any
business colleague who is, as well as the name of a reliable local

dealer. You may also find that your local education authority's adult studies programme includes the business use of spreadsheets.

2

A systematic approach

Successful turn round will normally involve two steps:

- Survival—a short-term action plan, or *survival plan*, drawing on whatever knowledge and information is immediately available.
- Recovery—a *strategy for recovery*, based on much more detailed fact-finding and analysis, leading to action plans which, if implemented correctly, will guide the company to a healthy and continuing future.

The strategy for recovery will be based on an in-depth analysis of the company and its market-place. A great deal of information is needed before this can be done and much of this information may not exist within the company right now. Just how much time will be needed to gather this information and complete the planning process will depend on how much of the necessary information does exist at present, how easy or how difficult it may be to gather the information that is missing and on whether or not you seek external help to share this workload.

Whatever time is needed for this it is likely to be measured in months rather than weeks. If the financial position of the company is very serious, it could, in fact, face closure or liquidation unless some remedial action is taken in a very much shorter time-scale. This is the rationale behind the survival plan. Even if the position is less serious and the time-scale less critical, common sense points to the benefit of making the maximum improvements in the short term.

The precise objectives you will seek from the two steps of survival and recovery will depend on just how bad a position the company is actually in at this point in time. If the losses are only marginal and fairly recent in origin, you may well find it feasible to seek to achieve break-even as a result of the survival plan itself and to envisage the strategy for recovery as the vehicle which will then guide the company to an acceptable level of profit.

In a more desperate and deep-rooted situation the survival plan may of necessity have to become more of a damage-limitation exercise, with break-even becoming the prime objective of the strategy for recovery. This is the scenario assumed in this book.

ANALOGY WITH A ROAD ACCIDENT

Throughout these steps of survival and recovery the company is going to be your 'patient' and the steps you will be taking will have a close parallel with the treatment needed by a victim of a serious motorway accident.

Whatever the cause of the accident, and regardless of who was to blame, someone has summoned the roadside emergency services. In this case that is you. You are now on the scene and faced with tangled wreckage, a great deal of bleeding, multiple fractures and possible internal injuries that you have no means of diagnosing at the roadside. To make matters worse, the patient is unconscious and cannot answer your questions. That may be an uncomfortably close analogy to the loss-making company you have recently arrived at.

Emergency Rescue Service

Your first step is to assess what emergency action is needed before removing the patient to hospital. Your first action is quite literally to stem the bleeding and put the limbs in splints. You are concerned at this stage only with keeping the patient alive until you can find out more about the injuries.

It is exactly the same with a loss-making business. At this stage the problem is far too time-critical to start with the logical process of detailed examination, analysis and diagnosis. You have to take emergency action just to keep the company alive. You have to staunch the bleeding very quickly before the money runs out. And you have to apply first aid to the limbs to prevent the company from becoming crippled for life.

Survival Plan

At this stage survival is the name of the game. You are very simply going to buy yourself some time in order to do a more thorough and more far-reaching job a bit later on. This will be your *survival plan*. Its objective is to keep your company alive until you can find out a great deal more about the real problems.

In the accident scene the next step is to remove the patient by ambulance to a hospital emergency ward, where a full range of life-support systems are available. Your own life-support system, once you put your survival plan into operation, is going to involve you in the daily monitoring of the company's progress, especially its cash flow, until you get the company back to a more stable condition.

Examination, Diagnosis and Prescription

With the accident victim in hospital and on a life-support system there begins the process of determining the full extent of the injuries. This will involve fact-finding. What has been damaged? Which bones are broken? What is the extent of any internal injuries? To this task will be applied all the skills of medical science. At this stage the main purpose is gathering information in order to make a correct diagnosis of the injuries. This has to be done before the correct treatment can be prescribed.

You will go through a similar process with your company. You will collect information and analyse this information in different ways until you understand the true nature and the full extent of the company's injuries. Only then will you be in a position to consider the alternative courses of action.

Once the hospital patient's injuries have been properly diagnosed, specialists will be consulted as to what treatment is required and how and when it is to be carried out. This treatment may very well involve surgery of some sort. It is important that the patient is first strong enough to survive surgery.

It is much the same with a sick company. Only when you have a full understanding of the real problems will you be in a position to consider the possible longer-term remedies. You will examine each and every injury or weakness and prescribe a cure for it. You too may have to consider surgery and, just like the hospital surgeon, you will have to ensure that the company is first nursed back to sufficient strength to be able to survive that surgery.

Constraints of Funding

In a very serious case the hospital staff may find that they are constrained by a lack of facilities. The funding of the National Health Service does not stretch to providing each and every hospital with all of the very latest and best equipment. It will be the same in your company's case and the constraint will be the very same—lack of funds.

In Britain you will almost certainly be better off in an NHS hospital if you have the misfortune to be injured in a motorway accident, but it would be very different indeed if it happened to you in many parts of the United States, for example. There, your chances of getting treatment in the best hospital may depend on whether or not you have private medical insurance.

The same analogy holds to some extent in your task of turning the company round. If it is your own company, or if it is privately-owned, you will be at the mercy of your bank manager. But if you are part of a larger group, you should have some reasonable expectation of financial support while you get the job done.

The Strategy for Recovery

These steps of examination, diagnosis and prescription of the treatment form the basis of the *strategy for recovery*. In the process of preparing this you will be going through most of the steps that a healthy and successful business would also go through if it sat down to the task of strategic planning for its future.

Treatment and Cure

An accident victim will clearly not recover unless the prescribed treatment is carried out with skill and care. This is the most important part of all. Afterwards the patient may need intensive care for some while, followed by a great deal of expert nursing and maybe some form of physiotherapy for a longer time afterwards.

It is exactly the same with your business. The strategy for recovery is an extremely vital step, but it will have been to no avail if you do not implement it professionally and skilfully. As you implement it you will need to have your finger on the company's pulse continuously over a long period. Even after you see all the signs of recovery you will do everything humanly possible to prevent a relapse; there will almost certainly be some aspects of the business that need careful massaging for a much longer period.

THE SYSTEMATIC APPROACH

The basic framework of this book closely follows that analogy of the motorway accident victim:

- Short-term *survival plan*
    - The situation appraisal:
      How bad is the position? (Chapters 3, 4)

How much time do you have? (Chapter 5)
- The survival plan (Chapter 6)
- Implementation and 'intensive care' (Chapter 7)
- Longer-term *strategy for recovery*
  - Questions concerning strategic direction (Chapter 8)
  - Detailed fact-finding (Chapters 9, 10, 11)
  - The strategy for recovery (Chapters 12, 13)

The strategy for recovery may lead you to a process of contracting onto a lower fixed-cost base. The key to such a restructuring is the subject of Chapter 14.

3

How bad is the position?

A realistic appraisal will be vital in every turn-round situation. If you are new to this company, it should be your highest priority task. The key questions to be answered at this stage are these:

- How bad is the position? In terms of business performance this question will be answered mainly by analysing the latest management accounts.
- How much time do you have? The amount of time you have before the 'life-support' systems switch off will depend on the state of your company balance sheet. It will also be influenced by whether this is a private company or whether it is part of a larger group, which is either cash-rich or vertically integrated.

THE IMPORTANCE OF MANAGEMENT ACCOUNTS

In this chapter and the next we shall address the first of these questions by studying the company management accounts. Before we do so there is a number of basic questions that must be asked concerning the accounts themselves:

- How frequently and how quickly should the accounts be available?
- What should you do if there are no accounts?
- What format should the accounts follow?
- What comparative data are needed?

There is also a number of checks and challenges to be made in order to ensure that the management accounts are in fact sufficiently reliable and will give a reasonably accurate indication of just how serious the present position is.

Frequency and Speed of Reporting

Without reliable management accounts on a regular basis you are in much the same position as a captain trying to steer his boat through the rocks blindfolded. It is more than likely that a company that is far behind with producing its management accounts will have a built-in delay to spotting problems and taking corrective action. This may well have been a factor leading to its present loss-making position.

You need, and must have, management accounts on a monthly basis. Computer systems have become both cheaper and more powerful over recent years and have removed the drudgery from financial and management accounting. Provided you have a reliable computer-based accounting system you should not have to wait much longer than about the tenth working day into the new month before the previous month's accounts are prepared. If this is not happening, then a high priority must be to reorganize the workflow and the priorities of work within the accounts department so that such a timetable can be achieved.

Well before that, within the first two or three working days of the new month, it should be possible for your accounts staff to produce a set of 'quick' figures, which will approximate to the final results. The difference between these figures and the final accounts should be limited to the effect of significant invoices for expense items received after the quick figures were prepared and which were not budgeted for.

What if There Are no Accounts?

If you do not have up-to-date management accounts available, then this is the action you should take:

- Call in your auditors and ask them to prepare a draft set of accounts for you immediately. Do not consider the expense involved. If your company does not have up-to-date accounts, the chances are that your own people will not deliver what you need with the necessary speed or accuracy. Be prepared to do this for a further month if necessary.
- Install a simple integrated accounting system on a PC as quickly as possible. Your auditors will advise you on the choice of a suitable accounting software package. Appendix 3 gives some advice which will help you implement such a system with the minimum of problems.

The Format of the Management Accounts

The format of your management accounts should resemble that shown in Table 3.1. In time you will refine that format to the one that helps you manage and control your business most easily and most meaningfully. If you are part of a larger group, you may be

Table 3.1   XYZ Company management accounts

Net sales revenue	145 678	145.7
Material cost of sales	55 358	55.4
Added value	90 320	90.3
Direct labour	34 484	34.5
Gross margin	55 836	55.8
Works overhead	52 891	52.9
Works contribution	2 945	2.9
Sales and distribution costs	25 118	25.1
Administration costs	19 322	19.3
Depreciation	4 567	4.6
Profit/loss before interest	(46 062)	(46.1)
Interest	7 508	7.5
Profit/loss after interest	(53 570)	(53.6)

constrained to work with the standard format prescribed at group level.

Table 3.1 is applicable to manufacturing industry. If you are in the distribution business, you would arrive at gross margin where added value appears on that example and you would incorporate direct labour with works overhead into a single element called warehousing cost. You would probably also separate sales and distribution into individual elements in the accounts.

Two columns are shown on Table 3.1. One is in pounds, the other in thousands of pounds, to one decimal place of thousands. You have a choice of presentation; whatever makes most sense to you is the best.

What Comparative Data Should Be Reported?

Across the page on your management accounts you can have a wide variety of columns of information to help you interpret the results and set them in context. There is no universally agreed format for this; you must avoid making the accounts indigestible by presenting too much information.

Correctly presented, this information is like a guide to navigation. It will tell you:

- Where you have come from
- The course you have followed
- Your present position
- How far off course you are

These are the essential guides to good navigation. With just a little degree of inference you can then also ascertain:

- Where you are now headed

One set of comparative data which will satisfy these requirements is this:

- Current month: actual: in the chosen monetary unit
- Current month: actual: as a percentage of turnover

- Current month: budget: in the same monetary unit
- Current month: variance from budget: as a percentage variance
- Current month: change: percentage change from same month last year
- Year-to-date: actual: in the chosen monetary unit
- Year-to-date: actual: as a percentage of turnover
- Year-to-date: budget: in the chosen monetary unit
- Year-to-date: variance from budget: as a percentage variance
- Year-to-date: change: percentage change from same month last year

You have ten columns of information to digest, but you have a wealth of information readily at your fingertips as a result. It may be that your chosen accounting package will not present information in this form at the press of a button. This is where it is invaluable to construct a simple spreadsheet to do this for you in a few minutes each month-end once the management accounts are available.

The comparisons with budget will be possible only if you already have budgets for the current year. If you are not familiar with annual plans and budgets, ask your accountant or auditors to recommend a good textbook on the subject.

Checks and Challenges

Now that you have management accounts available to you in an appropriate format, you should ask some pointed questions before beginning to interpret them. Do you believe them? How sure are you that the information is correct? It is prudent to anticipate nasty surprises and take account of these before going any further. At this stage you do not have enough spare time to go turning over every stone, but there are some fairly common traps which may be lurking. The short-list that follows is by no means exhaustive:

- Is the processing of purchase invoices up to date?

- When was the sales invoicing 'cut-off'?
- How big is the pipeline of customer credits?
- How has the material cost of sales been calculated?
- How accurate is stock checking?
- Is there 'shrinkage' in the stocks?

Is purchase invoice processing up to date?

Never assume that purchase invoices are being processed correctly. If they are not, then a warning bell may sound in the form of a long list of suppliers chasing you personally for payment of overdue invoices which your accounts staff cannot find on their purchase ledger. If that does happen, then it indicates a big problem.

It probably means that the costs given on the management accounts are underestimated because invoices have not been processed. If that is the case, then one day, when you knock the accounting systems into shape, the backlog will be cleared and just when you thought you had reached some stability, you will find instead a bigger loss than before. And you will most likely also find a tight-lipped accountant blaming it on the profligacy of big-spending managers.

When was the sales invoice cut-off?

Another check you should make is this. How many days into the new month did your accounts and production staff connive to count as part of the month just ended? A sure way to pad out the sales figures is to steal a few days from the next month. After all, these orders were supposed to have been shipped before the month-end, and it was just a bit of bad luck on the shopfloor that stopped them getting out on time. Sooner or later you will reach a month where the past catches up and delivers an unwelcome disaster.

Check the customer credit claim pipeline

Find out how big a backlog of customer credit claims are in the pipeline awaiting processing. If you are supplying large customers, especially Japanese companies or multinationals, you should assume that they will deduct their debit notes from their next payment to you. They can afford to take such pre-emptive action because they are bigger than your own company is. If you do have a lot of customer claims in the pipeline, then there is yet more bad news awaiting you when you finally streamline that part of the system and get it up to date.

These are some of the items that may simply have been 'overlooked' in the attempt to impress you by producing a set of accounts half-way towards the deadline you set. Next month, if the system catches up, you may be facing results that have deteriorated for no apparent reason.

Challenge material cost of sales calculations

The most important question you have to ask is this: How is the material cost of sales calculated? It may well be that there is a system that calculates this accurately, but your computer systems need to be fairly sophisticated for this to be the case.

If you do not have a computer system of proven accuracy, you can only really believe the material cost of sales figure if it is confirmed by a stock check. When was the last stock check carried out? The longer it is since the last one, the more important it is to go over this calculation with a fine tooth-comb. Challenge every assumption and then ask what adjustments had to be made after the previous half-dozen stock checks. That will give you a handle on the accuracy of the estimates.

In most companies there is too high a cost of taking stock each month. You either lose scarce and valuable production time or you get permanently hooked on double-time for weekend working. It helps enormously if you have a reliable formula for estimating material cost of sales by product group, which can be used in the months in between physical stock checks.

After you have queried the material cost of sales figure you may well have doubts about its validity; until you are certain of it you should assume that this figure has been understated rather than overstated, however unpleasant that may be in the present circumstances.

The importance of accurate stock checks

The need for good stock checks cannot be overemphasized, especially in a problem company. Too often material cost of sales can end up being the balancing item in the accounts. Accurate stock-taking is the only reliable way of eliminating that uncertainty.

One thing you should do is to insist on a stock check the month-end after you arrive. Not only that, you should supervise both the count and the evaluation yourself, and do the same on succeeding stock checks until you are sure that the material cost of sales is being reflected accurately in the accounts. Appendix 4 (page 247) gives a check-list of some basic prerequisites of good stock checking.

If you do the job thoroughly, you will find stock not previously recorded. You will also acquire a reasonable grasp of how much redundant or slow-moving stock you have, because the easiest place to find the cost price, if there are no recent receipts, is to refer back to the previous stock evaluation. You will then very quickly spot the items that have not moved since the last check.

It is only hands-on experience like this that will tell you what provisions you should be making against book value. We shall deal with that in Chapter 5. Another benefit of hands-on experience at this stage is that you will quickly gain a familiarity with material cost prices. This will be invaluable when you later get round to looking at product costings.

That very first time round the evaluation of stock should be done on a basis comparable with the previous stock check. After that, you may well decide to take a different and more conservative approach to valuation, but when you do so you must calculate the once-off effect of that in order to preserve comparability of your results.

Following a stock check, the calculation of material cost of sales since the previous stock check is as follows:

	opening stock
plus	purchases
minus	closing stock
equals	material cost of sales

Any difference between that figure and the estimated figure in the accounts is then either a compensating profit or a further loss. It is quite astonishing just how often the result is an addition to the loss.

Is there 'shrinkage' in the stocks?

Too many people put this down to 'shrinkage', while others suspect that their stock is 'walking'. If you really do believe that the latter could be the case, then you should get advice from a security expert as quickly as possible. If the 'shrinkage' was both real and significant, nipping it in the bud quickly will help stem the losses and this may buy you a little more time to solve the company's real problems.

Your materials will normally need to be intrinsically valuable and/or have a high value to volume or weight ratio to be 'accident-prone' in this way. For most of the time the stock loss is simply the result of inherent inaccuracies within the system, and more often than not it will be the outcome of using too optimistic an estimate of material cost of sales in between stock checks.

Your company's true trading position is very unlikely to be better than your management accounts suggest. The checks and challenges outlined in the last few pages may help you assess the downside risk of the trading position being substantially worse than you will infer from the accounts. It is best that you know this as early on as possible.

INTERPRETING THE ACCOUNTS

If you have comparisons with budget, the question 'how bad is the position?' will be partially answered by establishing how far off course the company is right now. This will answer the question only in very relative terms. It begs the question of how bad the position would have been if there was no variance from budget.

Expressing the loss as a percentage of turnover quantifies the answer in more absolute terms, but does not help explain the situation or identify what can be done to make improvements.

The most helpful answers will come from a detailed examination of the management accounts. Two questions are vital:

- Where in the accounts does the loss turn to profit?
- What is the break-even point?

Break-even point is the absolute definition of just how serious the present position actually is and is the subject of the next chapter. For the moment we can put things in more immediate perspective by seeing at what point in these management accounts the minus figure changes to a plus figure.

We must consider the different implications that follow depending on whether your accounts show black or red figures at the following levels in the management accounts:

- Before group charges
- Before interest
- Works contribution
- Gross margin
- Added value

Let us now take a much closer look at some management accounts (Tables 3.2, 3.3 and 3.4), which could be those of the XYZ Company from Table 3.1, but at a different point in its rise or fall.

Group Management Charges

Table 3.2 shows one item that may appear on your management accounts but was omitted from Table 3.1. If you are part of a

Table 3.2   XYZ Company management accounts

	£000
Net sales revenue	183.6
Material cost of sales	53.8
Added value	129.8
Direct labour	38.3
Gross margin	91.5
Works overhead	52.7
Works contribution	38.8
Sales and distribution costs	22.1
Administration costs	17.3
Depreciation	3.6
Profit/loss before interest	(4.2)
Interest	1.7
Profit/loss after interest	(5.9)
Group management charge	6.8
Profit/loss after group charge	(12.7)

larger group, there may be an additional line entitled group management charge. If there is, there are some critical questions you should ask:

• How much is this charge, expressed as a percentage of your total loss? If it is only a few per cent then forget it completely, but if it accounts for anything approaching half or more of your loss, as it does in Table 3.2, then it is in itself a major contributing factor to your company's losses and you must challenge it.

• What are you getting in return for this charge? If you are, in fact, getting some valuable and indispensable service from the

group, such as a debt collection service which keeps your
debtors tightly controlled, then be prudent in your challenge,
but do not give up.

- How is this charge calculated? The odds are that it is levied on
the basis of either turnover or head-count. You may have a
valid case for arguing that it should instead be levied on
ability to pay.
- Could you perform the same service in-company, but at a
lower cost? This could well be the case if group has padded
out the direct cost with some element of overhead recovery,
like rent and rates, for instance.
- Are you getting nothing very tangible in return for this
charge? The costs of your group central administration may

Table 3.3   XYZ Company management
accounts

	£000
Net sales revenue	191.4
Material cost of sales	54.9
Added value	136.5
Direct labour	38.6
Gross margin	97.9
Works overhead	49.1
Works contribution	48.8
Sales and distribution costs	21.1
Administration costs	17.3
Depreciation	3.6
Profit/loss before interest	6.8
Interest	9.7
Profit/loss after interest	(2.9)

simply be being apportioned out to the subsidiaries. The head office departments may be required to operate to a zero budget because they are not a true profit centre, so a charge is levied on you to recover their costs of operation.

The fact that they have to consolidate your company accounts into their group accounts, their main administrative task, has nothing whatever to do with the profitability or unprofitability of your company. If the group chooses to operate in this way, then that is their choice. If they were to close your company down, these central costs of administration would not reduce by one penny.

- Do the group levy this management charge for tax reasons? There may be a very sound reason for their doing so. If that is the case, then at least you should insist on preparing a separate set of accounts which omits management charges and which will be the real basis on which your own performance will be judged. If they are not persuaded, do it anyway. Once your company is making a profit before management charges they could not close this company without it having an adverse effect on the group's own results.

The Relevance of Interest Charges

Moving up your management accounts, are you making a profit before interest charges? If you are, as the XYZ Company is in Table 3.3, then you are probably less in need of help than you think. You clearly still have to improve your profit to cover the interest charges, but at least you have a potentially viable business. The main questions to ask at this stage are: What are you really paying for with these interest charges? Why has the overdraft or loan mounted to where it is today?

There are three possible explanations for this:

- Funding on-going losses
- Funding capital investment in the past
- Funding working capital at present

Funding losses

Loss-making companies end up with ever-increasing cumulative losses which have to be funded, usually by borrowing yet more money. This can be a particularly vicious spiral. Is the largest part of your interest simply the penalty you are paying for funding past losses? If you now have a respectable profit before interest, but are still funding losses from the past, then you have a millstone round your neck that you certainly do not deserve on the basis of present performance.

If that is so and it is your own business, or if it is a private company, you should be talking to a company or institution that specializes in providing tailor-made business finance packages for companies like yours. Your bank manager should be able to help you find the right one.

If you are part of a larger group, and particularly if you are new to the job, then you should argue very strongly to have this burden of debt removed at a stroke. The simplest method is for the parent group to increase your paid-up share capital by an amount equivalent to the borrowings. You then start with a clean slate.

Borrowing for capital investment

Next ask yourself how much of the borrowings are attributable to capital investment in recent years. If that is a significant element, and you have had to turn to borrowings because the company was not generating cash, then you are quite simply undercapitalized.

In a group situation it would be quite unreasonable for the parent group not to increase the paid-up share capital by a compensating amount, especially now that you have a viable operation. Even if the group is short of cash, it should at least be able to borrow more easily than you can, and the interest charges are going to do less damage to the group's consolidated accounts than they are now doing to your own.

If you do not have a group umbrella over your head, you should very definitely be looking to increase the equity in the business and reducing the debt. Are the shareholders able and willing to inject additional capital? If not, are they prepared to dilute their own shareholding and invite other investors? You should be asking your bankers or an investment bank for advice on the various options.

Funding working capital

If it is not past losses or capital investment, then probably the major part of your borrowings are being used to finance working capital. In that case it may be a little bit more difficult to reduce the burden you are carrying.

Public groups have varying attitudes to the financing of working capital. Some will simply aim to set up their subsidiaries according to a fixed debt/equity ratio. This will probably be the case where your company is only a trading company and where the assets of the business are owned by the parent group. At the opposite extreme some groups may decide that fixed assets should be funded by the shareholder (i.e. themselves) and working capital by borrowings. You may find a variety of policies between these two.

If you have the problem of financing working capital, then you need specialist advice. Before you go seeking that advice, however, make sure that you have your working capital properly under control. There are three aspects you must check in detail:

- Debtors. Are you on top of your debt collection? Will it really hurt your sales that much if you simply put the late payers on stop until they pay? You should not, at this stage, consider factoring your debts. You may very well consider this option later on in a different context, but for the moment your problem is the cost of finance. Factoring is going to increase the real cost rather than reduce it.
- Stocks. Are your stocks really tightly controlled? Have you tried reordering later and ordering less at a time? Can you find a supplier who will deliver to you on a JIT (Just-in-Time) basis?

- Creditors. What can you squeeze out of your suppliers? Have you asked for consignment stocks or a sale or return deal? Are you getting the best payment terms possible?

This is a glib overview of the larger subject of working capital control, but the point is that you will end up highly embarrassed if you seek help when your real problem is that your working capital is not properly managed in the first place.

Works Contribution

Moving still further up the management accounts, is there a positive works contribution, but not enough to cover the remaining overhead costs? The first column of Table 3.4 illustrates this. In this case you are covering all of your variable costs plus a significant element of your fixed costs. The position is bleak, but far from irrecoverable.

Table 3.4   XYZ Company management accounts

	£000	£000	£000
Net sales revenue	142.9	107.2	71.5
Material cost of sales	50.4	41.8	30.4
Added value	92.5	65.4	41.1
Direct labour	38.6	39.7	45.6
Gross margin	53.9	25.7	(4.5)
Works overhead	46.2	45.3	42.6
Works contribution	7.7	(19.6)	(47.1)
Sales and distribution costs	16.5	16.5	16.5
Administration costs	14.8	14.8	14.8
Depreciation	2.9	2.9	2.9
Profit/loss before interest	(26.5)	(53.8)	(81.3)
Interest	3.8	4.2	4.6
Profit/loss after interest	(30.3)	(58.0)	(85.9)

Gross Margin

Moving on to the middle column of Table 3.4 you will see that you now have to go as far back as gross margin before a plus figure appears. You are recovering not much more than your variable costs and the position is now rather more desperate.

By the time you reach the third and final column of Table 3.4 you will find a negative gross margin. You are not even covering your variable costs. A company in this situation has a very big problem indeed, and we shall need to find out a great deal more about this problem. The chances of survival will depend very largely on how much of the problem is due to underutilized production capacity rather than inherently low product profitability. We shall look at this in more depth in Chapter 4.

Added Value

Table 3.4 omits a column with negative added value. If added value is negative, that would mean that your selling prices were not even paying for the material content of the products you make. There is nothing left over to pay for the work done, let alone pay for any of the overhead costs.

If you find yourself in such a position, then your chances of surviving depend entirely on whether or not you have *any* products that actually do generate added value.

Using the motorway accident analogy, you will have no option but to perform an emergency operation at the scene of the accident and amputate the irrecoverable limbs in order to save your patient. Your only course of action is to opt for an immediate restructuring plan, and it may be best if you move right away to Chapter 14 in this book which will lead you through such a plan.

The chances of survival progressively lessen the further up the management accounts you have to go before a positive figure emerges. That is because the problem is deeper rooted. It will also take longer to produce corrective action. So much depends on time-scale; in Chapter 5 we shall relate this to the funds available.

What Else Can the Accounts Tell You?

This quick analysis of the management accounts has now given us a very broad-brush view of the seriousness of the present position. In Chapter 4 we shall examine the break-even point, which will add greater clarity to it. For the moment let us explore three other avenues that will add to our understanding of the problem:

- What are the current trends?
- What can be learned from the past?
- What can be inferred about the future?

These questions can be answered in part from the management accounts, but a little additional data will help fill in the bigger picture.

Analyse Trends in the Results

What is the current trend? Is the position deteriorating? If so, how rapidly is it deteriorating and why? To answer these questions you must be careful to distinguish between:

- Business performance trends
- Seasonal trends
- Cyclical trends

Trends in performance

From looking at previous months' management accounts you should be able to identify the current trend, both in sales and in costs.

To be able to account for this trend will need yet more questioning. If there was a budget, you will have a comparison against budget. If there is an adverse variance, you will have to ask whether the budget was credible to start with or whether things have truly slipped out of control. You will have the comparison with last year and you can begin to ask what has happened to account for the year-on-year change.

You will want to see a more detailed build-up of the numbers given against each line of cost headings on the management accounts, and preferably to see this related to the budget figure. It is only in this way that you will understand how costs have slipped out of control. In the last analysis you should demand to see actual invoices if no one can explain the cost variances.

Also, try to identify early on the 'dustbin' code used when the accounts staff are unsure of which expense code is applicable. It can often be works maintenance, which is one of the least controllable elements of cost and one where sudden increases in expense are frequently accepted with a shrug of the shoulder.

Seasonal trends

Study previous years' accounts to identify any seasonal trends, particularly around holiday months or Christmas, New Year or bank holiday periods, before you jump to the conclusion that you are on an up-trend or a down-trend. Visit your major customers and ask them what the major seasonal trends in their business are. Knowledge of their business pattern will help you understand your own much better. Be prepared for subtle variations in the seasonal trends from one year to the next.

Cyclical trends

If your business operates under the influence of a cyclical trend, this may be more difficult to identify until you gain more experience of the market you operate in. It is important to recognize the 'signposts' or early warning signs of an impending upturn or downturn. I lived in a cyclical market for over ten years and by the end of that time I understood pretty thoroughly what was driving the market, but could still not predict exactly when the next upturn or downturn was going to take place.

Seek out any statistician among your major raw material suppliers whose job it is to monitor your market. Such a person may help you understand very quickly the forces underlying any cyclical trends.

Where Have You Come From?

Take time at this stage to work out where the company has come from. Part of the answer will come from studying accounts of past periods, but it should be supplemented with some more research at this stage.

It helps to know how the company has arrived at its present position and for how long it has been in trouble, if only to go forward with a clearer understanding of the course of events. There may be past mistakes you can identify and resolve to avoid in future. Take whatever records are available and prepare on one sheet of paper the key events or milestones of the last 15 to 20 years.

Table 3.5 shows a very simple illustration. This is a company making instrumentation equipment, and although it was founded

Table 3.5   ABC Company milestones

Year	Turnover (£000)	Profit (£000)	Milestones
1978	402	31	First full year trading; Mr A is MD
1979	417	1	
1980	494	1	
1981	444	42	Mr A retires; Mr B takes over as MD
1982	?	(4)	
1983	?	(12)	Mr A dies in retirement
1984	?	(4)	Mr B resigns; Mr C takes over as MD
1985	?	15	
1986	720	0	
1987	760	1	Mr C resigns; Mr D takes over as MD
1988	990	(37)	
1989	1050	(50)	Mr D is fired

40 years ago, it was incorporated only in 1977. At that stage its founder, Mr A, was the majority shareholder and his long-standing partner, Mr B, owned one share.

All of the information in Table 3.5 has come from the data on file at Companies House. It is only a very bare skeleton of what really happened, but already it tells us a great deal. It tells us that it was a healthy company under the command of Mr A, and that it successfully weathered the recession of 1980. Unfortunately Mr A has since died and we cannot seek his advice.

We know that Mr B and Mr D were responsible during their respective tenures as managing director for a reversal into loss, and it would be useful to ask some of the longer-serving members of staff for their recollections of these periods so that we can perhaps avoid repeating their mistakes. Much more significantly, Mr C turned the company round in 1985. We do not know why he resigned, but if he can be located, this man may be worth listening to. It would appear that he was the architect of a period of growth after some years of static sales.

When you have to talk to the stakeholders—the employees, the customers, the suppliers and, most importantly, the bank mana-ger and the shareholders—you are not going to be able to avoid having the past thrown in front of you. You will at least be able to face these discussions with a certain degree of comprehension; this can only be to your benefit.

You should take the time to prepare a simple guide to the past, as I have illustrated. Your sources of information are the com-pany's annual reports and accounts and the minute book of the board meetings and AGMs. Even if the turnover is not disclosed in the annual accounts, you will almost certainly find it in the minute books. From the minute books you will learn a great deal if you have the patience to sift the wheat from the chaff, but do not spend too much time on it.

There will be a lot of boring detail, but it is unlikely that major decisions and major events will have passed by without having been recorded. You should be able to add milestones like exten-sions to factory space, introduction of new products and winning or losing of major contracts, some of the important flesh that the bare bones of the public records did not reveal in the company we saw in Table 3.5.

Where Are You Headed?

Returning to that navigational analogy, you now not only know where you are, you also have a fairly clear idea where you came from and what course the ship has followed up to this point. Right now, it is on automatic pilot and is an ungainly beast to steer. It is going to be slow to respond to your hand on the wheel, so you need to have a view as to where it is immediately headed.

This is the time to get the crystal ball out for an hour or so and ask the question: What is known about the short-range future? From the latest management accounts, together with your analysis of the current trends, you will have part of the answer. The current order bookings data will help add some precision.

The Significance of Order Bookings

Order bookings data are by far and away the most reliable guide to the coming periods and it is surprising how often this vital information is not available. There are many managers who claim to know the current value of their order book, usually by totting up the value of the works orders already issued to the shopfloor. They can equate that to so many weeks' production and so long as it hovers around the same level month after month, they believe all is well.

That is simply wishful thinking. Just suppose, for instance, that the production arrears have been increasing steadily for the last few months. How do you reconcile that to a stable order book? The answer, of course, is that the new order intake, the life-blood of the company, is actually decreasing.

There is no substitute for keeping an order register and insisting on having the value of new orders totted up daily, weekly and monthly. But you have to lay down strict rules as to what constitutes an order, otherwise you may find double-counting which makes the position appear better than it really is. There are three rules to lay down to avoid this:

- Only book firm orders covered by customers' written purchase order. If you book tentative or promised orders, then the bookings data will be invalid if the firm order is not subsequently received or, just as bad, if the order gets booked for a second time when the firm order is actually received. Be careful as well that you do not accidentally double-count orders received by fax when the customer has also sent the original to you in the post.

- Insist that all cancellations and amendments are recorded properly. Sales staff can be very reluctant to enter the bad news in the order register.

- If you are in the type of business where you have blanket orders for scheduled call-off, then you have to develop some arithmetic for ensuring that you calculate and record as accurately as possible the net increase or decrease in order value each time a new schedule comes in.

Let us now assume that you have valid order bookings data. Here is how it helps you predict the future. Suppose that, with no seasonal trend in your business and with a production lead-time of a nominal four weeks, your monthly invoiced sales over recent months have been as follows:

Invoiced Sales (£000)

Jan.	Feb.	Mar.	Apr.	May	Jun.
105	99	115	104	121	127

Looking at that trend in invoiced sales could be positively encouraging. The trend is unmistakably upwards and you would be likely to predict that the losses will reduce over the next few months.

Now look at your order bookings, or better still plot a graph of your sales and bookings figures. Suppose the bookings were as follows:

Order Bookings (£000)

Jan.	Feb.	Mar.	Apr.	May	Jun.
126	122	107	112	104	100

These figures present a totally different picture from the pattern of invoiced sales. The manager with the latter set of data is going to forecast a totally different result over the coming months than the one with only sales invoice figures to hand. It is the bookings data that will provide the most reliable guide to the coming months.

Later on, you may be able to develop a more sophisticated system which will take you one step further back in the sales cycle but which will enable you to see a few more months into the future. That will involve recording sales enquiries or quotations, and using that information to double-guess future months' order bookings, but it requires a very firm understanding of customers' time-scales and ordering habits.

A SHORT-RANGE FORECAST

With the order bookings data you should be able to make a reasonably accurate forecast for the next couple of periods ahead. This is important because it is unlikely that any decision you make, or any action you take, is going to alter significantly the out-turn very quickly.

There will be other data to hand, which you should take into account as well as the hard statistics of order intake:

- Are any major sales contracts known to be coming to an end over the coming months?
- Are there new sales contracts that the company has a high probability of winning?
- Are any price increases in the pipe-line?
- Is a wage review due?
- Is a rent review looming up?
- Are there any major quality problems that may have an impact on the next few months' results?

- Are any key staff leaving?
- How many production staff are taking holidays next month?

These are just a few of the key questions that you must take into account in shaping your forecast over the short range. It is vitally important that you consider all the downside risks and err on the conservative side. When you come to formulate your survival plan you are going to need to know not just where you are today, but where you are likely to be when the results of your plan begin to take effect.

With the help of your spreadsheet, you can now extrapolate forward from last month's management accounts, basing your short-range forecast on what is the known sales order position. You can then very easily do a 'what if?' calculation to show you the impact on this forecast of the other changes that are likely to take place in the immediate future.

4

The break-even point

BREAK-EVEN

The break-even point is the level of sales revenue at which sufficient gross margin is generated to cover the overhead costs of the business, including interest charges. Calculation of this break-even point will provide the clearest answer to that key question: How bad is the position? It will allow you to work out by how much sales revenue must increase before break-even is achieved. This is a very concise definition of the level of improvement needed over the months ahead and it will be a major consideration facing you when you begin work on the survival plan.

In this chapter we shall deal first with how the break-even point can be quickly calculated and then we shall examine in more depth a number of key factors that impact on it. The most important of these is the level of capacity utilization. In studying this we shall weigh up the arguments for and against reducing capacity to match the on-going level of demand.

The other factors which affect the break-even point are:

- Continuing losses needing funding
- Marginal pricing policies
- The product mix

In a loss-making position the combination of these factors often has the result of continually moving the break-even point higher and so further out of reach. This is the trap of the 'moving goal-posts'. Understanding the effect of this and keeping the break-even point within reach are critical to success.

Finally, we shall summarize what can be done to lower the break-even point and so set a more attainable target for the survival plan.

CALCULATION OF BREAK-EVEN POINT

We shall use the XYZ Company's management accounts given in Table 3.1 (page 26) to show how the break-even point can be calculated. There is a large raft of overhead costs which are mostly fixed costs. In the XYZ Company's case these overhead costs are as follows:

	£000
Works overhead	52.9
Sales and distribution	25.1
Administration	19.3
Depreciation	4.6
Interest	7.5
Total overhead costs	109.4

Break-even will be reached when sufficient gross margin is generated to pay for these overhead costs. If you adopted the comparative data recommended in Chapter 3, you will already have a column on your management accounts which shows each item on the accounts as a percentage of net sales revenue. In the case of the accounts given in Table 3.1 (page 26), the relevant figures would be as follows:

	£K	%
Sales revenue	145.7	100.0
Material costs	55.4	38.0
Added value	90.3	62.0
Direct labour	34.5	23.7
Gross margin	55.8	38.3

The calculation of break-even is then done as follows: divide the overhead costs by the gross margin percentage, and the result is the break-even point. With the figures we are now working on that calculation looks like this:

$$\frac{109.4}{38.3} \times 100 = £K286$$

The break-even point is £K286 per month. That means you virtually need to double your monthly sales in order to break even—a fairly daunting prospect indeed. But the position may not be quite so bad as that.

THE EFFECT OF CAPACITY UTILIZATION

The chances are that right now there are more people employed as direct labour operatives on the shopfloor than are really needed, especially if the sales figures have taken a dramatic downturn within the recent past. If that is so, then you will be able to support an increase in sales without the need for hiring additional labour. In other words, you may be able to grow your sales while holding direct labour costs at a constant level for some time. You are in effect operating well below your current level of production capacity.

Conventional wisdom at this point says that if that is the case, you should be making the excess staff redundant, thereby reducing both costs and losses without further ado. This is a matter where you will have to exercise some fairly fine judgement. If you were to find that by doing so the savings were so significant as to make a major dent in the losses, then clearly you should follow that course of action. Later on we ought to be able to find ways of tackling the rest of the problem without the need for such a massive increase in sales as the break-even calculation suggests.

But just look again at the example we used. In this case, even if *all* of the direct labour force were terminated, there would still be a loss of almost £20 000 a month, and there would be no production capacity left afterwards. In this case I would advise you to keep your nerve and postpone any decision until you are putting together your survival plan. By then the position may look different.

If the survival plan does envisage new sales growth, then you may in fact need all of your direct labour force to cope with the increase in production. The last thing you need is to find that you are unable to recruit additional skilled staff just as the order book builds up, especially if you are located in an area where recruitment is difficult.

In a month's time you will also have a better idea of how your managers judge their staff. You might find today that they do not approach this quite as objectively as you would wish. A little more time will help you identify who should go and who should stay.

What Is the Real Break-even Point?

Since you have a lot of spare capacity let us look on the direct labour force, for the time being at any rate, as part of the fixed costs to see what difference that makes to the break-even calculations. The fixed costs will then look like this:

	£000
Direct labour	34.5
Works overhead	52.9
Sales and distribution	25.1
Administration	19.3
Depreciation	4.6
Interest	7.5
Total fixed costs	143.9

In this case, the break-even point is arrived at by dividing these costs by the percentage added value (see page 51) instead of the gross margin percentage:

$$\frac{143.9}{62.0} \times 100 = £K232$$

That new break-even figure of £K232 is very significantly lower than the figure of £K286 we first calculated. You need only to increase sales by 60 per cent instead of doubling them, a somewhat more feasible but still difficult task.

We did, however, make the assumption that direct labour costs were fixed when we made this calculation. Do you in fact have sufficient production capacity to support sales of £K232? One way to find out would be to ask your production manager. There may be a reluctance to concede that much more than a token percentage increase can be achieved. Production managers do not like being put on the spot in this way and may not have the detailed information necessary to calculate exactly what full capacity means in terms of sales value, especially if you are in a jobbing shop type of business.

The safest method is to back-track through previous months' sales and production data and find out what level of production the present direct labour complement has actually achieved before. If you have good data on site, you may be able to plot a graph showing a relationship between numbers employed and production value.

In this example, let us suppose we find that for several months, not too long ago, but before the fairly dramatic decline in the order book took place, the monthly sales were frequently up in the £K180–90 band and that the numbers employed have remained the same since then.

One thing is now crystal clear. You will need to hire some more people in order to reach the break-even point of £K232. This in turn will increase the direct labour costs and you will need to do the calculations all over again. You are looking at a sort of iterative calculation and this may be the moment to build a model on your spreadsheet to help make this calculation more manageable.

The Best Approximation

Let us do it in a simpler way. If you are reasonably sure that you could again sustain sales in the region of £K180–90 a month, let us assume that production capacity is £K185, the average of that bracket of figures. At that level of sales the direct labour costs will be £K34.5, the same actual pounds figure as at present, but it will then represent only 18.6 per cent of sales revenue instead of the higher figure of 23.7 per cent which appears on the current management accounts. Material cost of sales will stay as a constant percentage, but the gross margin percentage will change for the better:

	Sales of £K145	Sales of £K185
Material costs	38.0%	38.0%
Direct labour	23.7%	18.6%
Gross margin	38.3%	43.4%

If you now divide this revised gross margin of 43.4 per cent into the original overhead costs of £K109.4, you will find that this gives a break-even point of £K252. You will need a 73 per cent increase in sales to break even, more than we imagined a few minutes ago, but still more attainable than the figure we first arrived at.

Of all the figures we have looked at thus far, this is the one that best quantifies the answer to the question: How bad is the position?

What we have done is to arrive at an approximately correct break-even figure. You could spend a great deal of time trying to quantify capacity in more detail in order to arrive at a more exact figure. Along the way you would probably come to a great many intangibles and make more than one error in the process. You should always bear in mind that it is better to be approximately correct than perfectly wrong.

THE 'MOVING GOAL-POSTS'

The break-even point is like a set of goal-posts. Over the coming months, as you go about implementing the survival plan, you and your team are going to be in the position of needing to score a winning goal fairly and squarely between these goal-posts.

Unfortunately, these particular goal-posts have a nasty tendency to move further out of reach once the game is in progress, and this can be more than a little disconcerting if you are not alert to this trap in advance.

The Effect of On-going Losses

The company's on-going losses will move the break-even point further away from you. Because the cumulative loss will be mounting up each month over the short-range future, so will the overdraft. That means that interest charges will also increase. Even if nothing else in the business changed, the interest would continue to increase and on a compound basis.

In the case of the XYZ Company in Table 3.1 (page 26), if the rate of interest on the overdraft were 16.5 per cent, then the monthly interest charge would increase by around 9 per cent every month, thus getting progressively higher as the compounding effect bites harder.

By the end of a full year the cumulative effect of this vicious spiral will be to move the break-even point a further 5 per cent out of reach. And that is before you take account of other possible increases in costs, such as wage reviews. You would then need at least a 5 per cent increase in selling prices just to stand still. To put that in perspective, it is a higher percentage increase than many companies were able to get from their major customers during the years of low inflation in the mid-eighties.

Marginal Pricing

Marginal pricing is the next factor that can extend the break-even point upwards. It is worth while exploring this subject in greater detail, because there may be short-term benefits of adopting marginal pricing tactics. The net effect will always be the following paradox:

- Reduce losses in the short-term.
- Raise break-even point to a higher level.

We have already seen that breaking even is all about generating sufficient gross margin to cover the overhead costs of the business. A number of things follow from that. The first is that for every £1 of additional gross margin generated, the loss will reduce by an equal amount of £1, provided there is no need to add to overhead costs in the process.

Even better still, for as long as you are working below the limit of capacity, then for every £1 of added value generated you will reduce the loss by £1.

This means that you could accept additional business at a lower price and still be helping to reduce the loss. If you use the mechanism of price to generate additional business, by lowering the price and by undercutting your competition, that will be a marginal pricing tactic. It should have a beneficial effect on the short-term results.

If your business is one where your main sales are in the form of once-off contracts, this is a potentially very beneficial tactic indeed. If you follow a policy of marginal pricing, you will at least gain the advantage of some short-term reduction of the losses and so buy yet a little more time to help solve the main problems, and you will still leave your pricing options open as far as the longer-term future is concerned.

On the other hand, if your typical sales are not once-off contracts but longer-term contracts, where you are committing yourself to accepting repeat business for months or even years to come, you should think very deeply about the possible longer-term consequences of such a policy.

One day in the not too distant future you may find these marginal prices unattractive. If that happens, you can be sure of an unsympathetic response from customers when you try to persuade them to accept an increase in selling price to 'a more economical level', the phrase most often used in such circumstances. The response will be especially unsympathetic where the customer is manufacturing a high-volume, price-sensitive product, like a motor car or a microwave oven, for example.

Let us look in more detail at what might happen if you use marginal pricing tactics. As before, we shall use Table 3.1 as the starting point. Suppose that you retained all of the existing business, currently worth £K145 a month. And suppose that you were able very quickly to generate a further £K45 of new business, but that you did this by discounting prices by 15 per cent. Then suppose that some of your existing customers found out that prices were being discounted and that you had to concede the lower price on a quarter of your existing business as well.

Taking that scenario yields a sales level of £K185 a month. By coincidence that is equal to what we previously had established as being the limit of production capacity. A very natural reaction would be to interpret that as good news, meriting the all-out effort needed to bring the works back to the target level of efficiency.

The likelihood is that there would be a nasty surprise lying ahead. The production manager is fairly certain to decide before the first week of the month has passed that the workforce needs to be increased by about 7 per cent to cope with the higher workload, and the production manager is likely to add a contingency for safety's sake. If you were the general manager, you would probably be faced with a request for 10 per cent additional staff. Your immediate reaction is easy to imagine.

You would remind the production manager that a production value of £K185 has been achieved with this same labour force several times before, and not that long ago either. But after one week, and being a realist, you would see all too clearly that the production manager was not going to achieve the production target you set. So, rather than jeopardize the hard-won sales, you would most probably relent and take on more staff.

The question you would then be asking at your next management meeting is: What on earth has gone wrong?

The Effect of Sales Mix

To make it easier to answer this we shall now look upon this business as comprising two distinct product groups. Product group A is the business transacted at the old price; that is now going to amount to three-quarters of the previous sales of £K145, i.e. £K109 a month. Product B will have a unit selling price 15 per cent lower than that of product A, and in this product group the sales will include one quarter of the previous sales, i.e. £K36, but discounted by 15 per cent thus making it only £K31 a month, plus the new business of £K45 a month, giving a total of £K76 for product B.

Although the price of product B has been discounted by 15 per cent, the costs of materials and direct labour per unit of sale have not decreased, so material cost and direct labour will have increased in percentage terms by a factor of 100/85. On product B

the material cost will now be 44.7 per cent of revenue and direct
labour will be 21.9 per cent. A summary of the gross margin will
look like this:

| | Product A | | Product B | | Total |
	%	£K	%	£K	£K
Sales revenue	100.0	109.0	100.0	76.0	185.0
Material cost	38.0	41.4	44.7	34.0	75.4
Direct labour	18.6	20.3	21.9	16.6	36.9
Gross margin	43.4	47.3	33.4	25.4	72.7

The corresponding management accounts are shown in
Table 4.1, and the assumption has been made in this example that
the previous month's loss had been funded by a reduction in working capital, thus allowing the interest charge to remain the same.

Seeing these accounts, the immediate reaction would be to key
in to the good news they present. The bottom-line loss has been
reduced by a third. The accounts would vindicate the production
manager; more people were needed but the good news is that the
direct labour costs increased by only 7 per cent. The temptation at

Table 4.1   XYZ Company after two months

	Before (£000)	After (£000)	Change (%)
Sales revenue	145.0	185.0	+28
Material costs	55.4	75.4	+36
Direct labour	34.5	36.9	+7
Gross margin	55.8	72.7	+30
Fixed costs	101.9	101.9	
Loss before interest	(46.1)	(29.2)	−37
Interest	7.5	7.5	
Loss after interest	(53.6)	(36.7)	−32

this stage would be to interpret these accounts as proof that marginal pricing is the answer to the company's problems.

A more detailed study of the figures will lead to a very different interpretation. The biggest contributory factor to the improvement was simply that all that underutilized capacity has now been soaked up. There has also been a disproportionately high increase in material costs: that is the most alarming feature.

Let us now see what would happen if we projected these figures through a further £K65 worth of additional sales, all of them also taken at the discounted price. This is a purely academic exercise because we shall assume that overhead costs remain the same. This is unlikely to be true as sales increase from £K145 to £K185 and then to £K250 a month. We shall again assume that enough is squeezed out of working capital to fund a few more months' losses; that way interest charges yet again remain unchanged.

The real outcome would have been significantly worse than the figures that appear in Table 4.2 because overhead costs could not have remained at the previous level. Despite this the example serves to make two points:

- Now that there is no more excess production capacity, direct labour costs are increasing at the same rate as material costs.
- There is still a loss showing on the bottom-line.

Cast your mind back to the best estimate we made of the break-even point. We calculated then that break-even point was £K252 and yet here we are, in Table 4.2, virtually there as near as makes no difference, yet still showing a loss.

To understand what has happened we must now calculate the gross margin percentage from the accounts summary given in Tables 4.1 and 4.2 and then make a new calculation of the break-even at these sales levels using those revised gross margin percentages.

This is what has happened as we moved from sales of £K145 to £K185 and then to £K250, using a marginal pricing policy to generate increased sales:

Sales revenue	£K	145.0	185.0	250.0
Gross margin	%	43.4	39.3	37.8
Break-even	£K	252.0	278.0	289.0

The break-even point has moved further and further out of reach at each step. It illustrates very clearly those moving goal-posts. The direct effect of marginal pricing brings bottom-line improvements in the short run, but at the same time it raises break-even point to a still higher level of sales revenue.

Most people who adopt a marginal pricing policy sooner or later have second thoughts as to the wisdom of their action. In very simple terms you are having to work harder all the time to produce each £1 of sales revenue; that is really a step in the wrong direction.

The example we looked at also demonstrates how the break-even point is sensitive to product mix. We have seen very clearly that increasing the proportion of a lower-margin product in the total mix has the effect of pushing the break-even goal-posts back still further.

The converse is also true. If you increase the mix of higher-margin products, then the break-even goal-posts will come closer within reach.

Table 4.2   XYZ Company after a few more months

	Before (£000)	After (£000)	Change (%)
Sales revenue	185.0	250.0	+35
Material costs	75.4	104.5	+38
Direct labour	36.9	51.1	+38
Gross margin	72.7	94.4	+30
Fixed costs	101.9	101.9	
Loss before interest	(29.2)	(7.5)	−74
Interest	7.5	7.5	
Loss after interest	(36.7)	(15.0)	−59

Later we shall see that eliminating the low-margin products completely from the product mix may be the surest way of attaining a break-even position.

Break-even will be achieved by one of the following actions; or by a combination of them:

- Increasing sales towards break-even point
- Reducing the break-even point

HOW TO LOWER THE BREAK-EVEN POINT

The ways in which the break-even point can be reduced are:

- Reducing the overhead costs.
- Improving the gross margins. An increase in selling price will improve gross margin. So too will reductions in material costs or direct labour costs.
- Making the product mix richer by increasing the proportion of higher-margin products in the sales mix.

5

How much time do you have?

The immediate situation appraisal posed two key questions. Over the last two chapters we have answered the first question: how bad is the position? That puts some measure against the level of achievement now needed.

The second question was: How long do you have before the life-support systems switch off? That will establish the time-scale available to you to reach that higher level of achievement. To answer this second question we must now look very carefully at your cash flow and your balance sheet.

So long as the business continues to generate losses it will require additional funding each month and any funding provided by means of an overdraft or loans must be secured against the assets of the business. We shall examine this subject in three steps:

- How long will the existing funding last? We shall answer this by studying cash flow and by making a forward cash flow projection based on the short-range forecast you prepared in Chapter 3.
- Can the funding be topped up? This will depend on whether or not your balance sheet identifies assets greater than the present level of funding. At that point we shall consider what the different implications are, depending on whether your company is privately owned or is part of a much larger group.
- Can the balance sheet be improved? If it can, this may enable additional funding to be secured.

Before leaving the subject of the balance sheet, we shall consider whether there are any provisions you should be making against book values.

HOW LONG WILL EXISTING FUNDING LAST?

The answer is related much more to cash and to cash flow than it is to simple profit or loss. In the final analysis profit or loss is a paper figure. You use it to measure performance; it is the basis for your liability to pay corporation tax; and it is one of the factors determining the share price or net worth of a business.

In the real world, however, it is the generation or consumption of cash and the availability of money to a business which have the greater impact on prospects in the immediate future. This is a lesson that all street traders learn on their first day and their example is well worth examination.

The Example of the Street Trader

Stop and take a closer look at a street trader's operations for a moment, especially one who sells fruit and vegetables, or anything else that will perish after a shelf-life of just one day. The most important thing is that this is a cash business. The trader will have paid for the stock in cash, it is sold for cash and the rent collector appears each day and gets paid in cash.

As trading hours draw to a close the street trader will be constantly making remarkably precise mental calculations, as if by second nature, of the mathematical odds of finding the selling price at which enough people will buy in order to ensure that no stock is left at the end of the day.

At the end of trading the difference between what money there was at the beginning of the day and what is left at the end of day is both profit and cash flow. It is almost always a profit and it goes straight to the bank. It is a real-time business.

The difference with your business is that there is an offset from real-time. For a start, you buy and sell on credit, and your management accounts reflect the point of sale or purchase and not the point of payment. You charge in your accounts for production materials when they are consumed, not when they are acquired. Capital investment is charged to the accounts, not as one big lump sum, but in the form of depreciation over the expected life of the investment. You make an accrual for invoices you should have received but have not, and major items like rent are treated as a prepayment and are charged to the accounts in equal instalments over the periods to which they relate.

This makes sense, because it enables a rational separation to be made between profit or loss on the one hand, and assets and liabilities on the other. It helps separate the performance of the business from the worth of the business, and above all it helps provide a picture of business performance that is truly comparable from one month to the next. The street trader working in real-time does not need management accounts. You do, and we have already looked at them in some depth.

The danger is that you concentrate primarily on what the management accounts tell you and look at the cash flow, the real-time part of your business, as an afterthought. It is like checking your engine oil after you garage the car for the night rather than checking it before you begin the day's journey.

A Cash Flow Statement
A simple statement of cash flow will look like this:

	Trading profit or loss
plus	Depreciation
plus or minus	Change in working capital
equals	Cash flow

This is a measurement of the cash generated or consumed by the trading over the period in question. In your case, since your company is making losses, it is likely to indicate an on-going cash consumption. The exception will be if you are able to squeeze out a reduction in your working capital. This is an extremely important point to which we shall return shortly.

This cash flow statement is not to be confused with a statement headed 'Source and Application of Funds'. That is an extension of the cash flow, which also takes account of any assets you buy and sell, as well as any changes to the funds provided to the business. You must not become confused between cash flow and funding. Funding is the big pot of money; cash flow is what flows in and out on a regular basis. Both are equally important to our discussions here and now.

The Cash Flow Forecast

At this point you should start using your spreadsheet yet again. Go back to the short-range forecast you made in Chapter 3 (page 47) and now project your additional cash needs over the immediate future. Make sure you show both the actual and the cumulative needs at the end of each period. We shall use these projections shortly.

In the case of the XYZ Company in Table 3.1 (page 26), such a projection may look something like this (the figures are in £000):

Future period	1	2	3	4	5
Cash needs: period	49	51	51	44	39
Cash needs: cumulative	49	100	151	195	234

How much time you have at your disposal to give emergency aid to your company is quite simply going to depend on how long it will be before the level of money in that big pot reaches the bottom, given that projection of cash consumption and whether or not you can succeed in getting the pot of money topped up along the way.

You can do some immediate calculations. Have you reached the limit of your overdraft facilities? If not, look very closely at that projection of cash consumption. At which month in the future does the cumulative cash requirement exceed the balance available on the current overdraft?

Let us recap on the XYZ Company situation. Suppose there is an agreed overdraft facility of £K500 and that the current overdraft stands at £K290. That means there is a further £K210 that can still be called on.

You can now revise the cash flow projection to include the funds remaining:

Future period	0	1	2	3	4	5
Cash needs: period		49	51	51	44	39
Cash needs: cumulative		49	100	151	195	234
Funds remaining	210	161	110	59	15	−24

What this indicates is that, provided everything goes according to forecast, then the pot of money runs out half way through the fifth month from now.

CAN THE FUNDS BE TOPPED UP?

If the funding available will last only a very few months, as in the example we have just seen, that may not allow sufficient time in which to bring about the necessary dramatic improvement in business performance. The question of whether or not the funds can be topped up will then become crucial to survival.

This is where the implications of ownership have a major bearing on the availability of additional funding. Let us first consider what the attitude of a parent group to this problem might be.

Parent Group Thinking

The provision of new funding should be very much easier to obtain if your company is part of a larger group, especially if the subsidiary you are managing is an integral part of the parent group's wider business activity. This means that your time-scale, although important, is not nearly as critical as it would be if you did not have this umbrella over your head.

It is unlikely that any respectable holding group would merely

let a subsidiary go to the wall. But in the last resort they will, if all
else fails, have to consider the closure of this problem-child. If that
decision is reached, closure should take place in an orderly
manner, with the rights of both employees and creditors being
respected.

What you have to take an early fix on is just what calculations
are being made in the group boardroom. Already they will be
asking you how long it will be before you break even, and you
may not know the answer to this until after you have finished
preparing the survival plan.

Most of the impartial advice being offered to you may be
suggesting that you will need to put in six months', twelve
months' or in a bad case perhaps even as much as two years' hard
work before you turn the corner. Back at group head office they
will be thinking in terms of a half or even a quarter of that time.

Closure Costs vs. Continuing Funding

The parent group's attitude will depend on the trade-off between:

- Costs of closure
- Cash consumption through to break-even

Someone at group head office will already have calculated what it
will cost to close the subsidiary down completely. This will
include redundancy payments, the loss on the sale of the assets of
the business and some provision for getting out of obligations such
as leases on property or equipment. You should do this calculation yourself, although there may be tax implications which will
reduce the real cost of closure from a group stand-point that you
may not be able to estimate.

The next calculation the group will make is how much funding
is going to be needed to see this problem-child through to
break-even. This will be the total projected cash consumption
over the periods from now until the break-even is predicted. This
is a calculation you should also make yourself.

They will then compare the cost of closure to the funding

needed to see you through to break-even. If it will require less cash to close the company, then time is running out very fast for you. You would be well advised to examine these calculations yourself each month-end to help you see the decision-making process as closely as possible through the eyes of your group board.

The chances are that the group board will weigh the two opposing costs on the balance-scale each and every time they meet. Once you are more in control of the situation you will be in a better position to give them your forecast of how far off the expected break-even point is. You then have to consider very carefully indeed the possible implications of this forecast when making it. Your estimates of any new investment needed for the business to attain break-even will be added into the equation as well.

The hard arithmetic is likely to be tempered by two other considerations:

- How much do they need your company? If you are part of an integrated group, then closure of your company could well have an adverse financial impact on results elsewhere in the group. This is not a valid reason for your continuing losses, but it may extend the time at your disposal.
- What will break-even do to the group results? When this ailing subsidiary does get back into the black it may result in a fairly considerable improvement in the parent group's own results. In some cases it could lead to a much greater increase in group profit than might accrue from organic growth in the profitable companies within the group.

To sum up, in a parent group situation you should be able to double-guess the time you have available by weighing up the costs of closure against the costs of remaining open for business. Provided the answer makes financial sense in terms of cash flow, you should not have to worry about the big pot of money not being topped up from time to time.

The Private Company's Problem

If your company does not have the benefit of a parent group umbrella over its head, then you are in a very different ball-game indeed. You almost certainly do not have a large pot of cash at this point in time. Much more likely, you will already have a substantial overdraft and the bank will have a fixed or floating charge on all or part of the assets of the company.

What, then, are the prospects of securing any additional funding which the cash flow projection indicates will be needed? The answer is quite simply that it depends on the state of your balance sheet. You are at the mercy of your bank manager.

The Balance Sheet

If you are not familiar with a balance sheet and how to interpret it, then before going any further you should get your accountant to explain this to you. Alternatively, you could call in at a local bookshop, where you will almost certainly find a paperback that will give you a broad enough grasp of the subject for our present purposes.

We shall now look at the example of a real company, which had many years of profitable trading behind it, but went into the red about two years ago. Over the last twelve months it has made a loss of £K211. Table 5.1 shows the balance sheet of a year ago and as it is today. This company has no long-term loans or provisions for deferred taxation, in other words nothing below the line of total assets less current liabilities; we shall ignore the small change held in the petty cash box.

You can see one significant change that has taken place over the last year. The loss has had to be funded by increasing the overdraft. This item is included as a creditor because it is repayable on call. The net result is that the company now has negative net current assets and its profit and loss account is very sadly depleted.

Suppose that this company were to repeat this loss of £K211 over the next full year and that nothing else changed. The balance

Table 5.1   ABC Company balance sheet (£000)

	Today	One year ago
Fixed assets	127	127
Current assets		
stock	225	209
debtors	219	227
	444	436
creditors	453	234
Net current assets	(9)	202
Total assets less current liabilities	118	329
Capital and reserves		
share capital	50	50
P & L account	68	279
	118	329

sheet at the end of the next year would then be as it appears in Table 5.2.

Something even worse has now happened. There is now a deficit on the profit and loss account and, because this deficit is greater than the share capital, it means that the total of capital and reserves—the shareholders' funds—also shows a deficit. This is matched by a negative total asset value.

Do the Assets Justify the Overdraft?

A year ago this company would have had relatively little difficulty in securing the funds it needed. Today it is much more doubtful. At the very best it cannot borrow enough to last any length of time unless a fairly dramatic turn round can be engineered. Before the next year-end the bank would almost certainly be calling in the overdraft and the receivers would be in.

Table 5.2   ABC Company balance sheet (£000)

	One year forward	Today	One year ago
Fixed assets	127	127	127
Current assets			
stock	225	225	209
debtors	219	219	227
	444	444	436
creditors	664	453	234
Net current assets	(220)	(9)	202
Total assets less current liabilities	(93)	118	329
Capital and reserves			
share capital	50	50	50
P & L account	(143)	68	279
	(93)	118	329

Coming back to the question of how long you have, there is one important point you should bear in mind. The overdraft facility you already have access to will have been secured by granting the bank a charge on the assets of the business.

If the remaining overdraft facility is greater than the total assets showing on today's balance sheet, then there are in fact insufficient assets to cover this, and you may well have less time than you calculated, especially if the bank is aware of the current position. On the other hand, if you have sufficient assets to cover this and still more, then you may have the possibility of an extension to your time-scale.

If things are indeed this close to the wind, you will again have to use your spreadsheet and project forward not only your cash flow, but also your balance sheet. The time available to you runs out when the shareholders' funds are exhausted, so you should be continuously forecasting just how many months away you are from this dreaded moment.

HOW TO IMPROVE THE BALANCE SHEET

Improving the state of the balance sheet and increasing the net asset value will have the net effect of justifying more funding and thus buying you more time. Every additional week or month of extension could be vital. There are ways of achieving this, but they may not all be practical possibilities in individual cases:

- Revaluation of assets
- Conversion to long-term loans
- Reduction of working capital
- Utilization of tax losses

Revaluation of Assets

Your company may be in the fortunate position of owning a freehold property. How long is it since you last had this revalued by your surveyor? In times of escalating property prices you may be surprised just how much this could have appreciated in value. The increase in value from the previous valuation will be an addition to your assets.

For example, suppose you were in the position of the company we have just looked at, and that there was a revaluation of property from £100 000 to £350 000—an increase of £250 000. That would make an enormous difference to your balance sheet. Table 5.3 shows what the position would now be.

At a stroke, the threat of the axe falling has been removed and some badly needed time has been acquired. The balance sheet is still not a healthy one. There are negative current assets and this will be a cause for concern to some trade creditors, but there will now be sufficient assets to justify the topping up of the pot of funds well through the immediate future.

The same could apply even if you have a leasehold only of the land, but own your own buildings. Again, get a surveyor in to

Table 5.3   ABC Company balance sheet (£000)

	One year forward	Today	One year ago
Fixed assets	377	377	127
Current assets			
stock	225	225	209
debtors	219	219	227
	444	444	436
creditors	664	453	234
Net current assets	(220)	(9)	202
Total assets less current liabilities	157	368	329
Capital and reserves			
share capital	50	50	50
revaluation reserve	250	250	0
P & L account	(143)	68	279
	157	368	329

revalue these buildings and see what difference it makes to your total asset position.

At this point you may be tempted to consider the sale and leaseback of any freehold land or property. The attraction of this is that the proceeds of the sale would then enable you to repay the bank overdraft. As a result, your creditors would reduce by the amount of the overdraft, and in the example we just looked at, this would then give you positive net current assets, both today and also at a point one year in the future. You can verify this on your spreadsheet by doing a 'what if?' calculation. The resulting balance sheet will look a whole world different.

In your position I would keep this trump card up my sleeve for just a little while longer. For a start, the lease payments or rent will add to your monthly costs, although this may be more than offset by the reduction in interest charges. That will largely depend on just how high the current rate of interest is.

The critical factor is that you will be entering into a lease which will run for anything from 10 to 25 years into the future. Until we start thinking about the strategy for recovery you should avoid making this commitment. You may well decide later on that this present site is not the right one for you; by retaining your freehold for the moment you keep that option fully open.

Are there any other items on your balance sheet which are undervalued, like stock or debtors, for example? You may well find that stock has been undervalued in the past in order to reduce profit for tax reasons. You may have found stock which had been 'lost' in the past. There may be specific provisions for bad debts which have now been either recovered or written off.

Some of this advice may strike you as being 'creative accounting'. That is a term you would certainly use if a public company manipulated its assets in order to overstate profit because the directors had a personal interest in manipulating the share price. That is not what we are concerned with here. We are talking about survival and your employees, customers and suppliers alike are all going to be better served if you win that battle for survival.

In the vast majority of cases you will not be fortunate enough to benefit from a revaluation of your assets. If the opportunity existed the chances are that, with a company in trouble, your predecessors will have exploited that tactic to the very full in previous years. So what else can you do?

Conversion to Long-term Loans

If you are part of a larger group, then you could argue to have some part of your borrowings converted into a loan that has a repayment date more than a year into the future. That would not alter your total asset value, but it would improve your current asset value. That would at least improve your creditworthiness in the eyes of most trade creditors, and if they have been hounding you, then you could remove that threat for a while by this tactic.

If you do have substantial freeholds or leaseholds, then you could consider taking out a straightforward commercial mortgage on these as opposed to using them to secure your bank overdraft. You would need the cooperation of your bankers, but the result would be to convert a short-term loan into a long-term loan, with the same benefits as I have just described.

Reduction of Working Capital

The other way in which you can buy a little more time is to squeeze your working capital. You can do this in three ways:

- Reduce debtors
- Reduce stocks
- Increase trade creditors

That will have the net effect of turning your working capital into money. It will help top up the funds, which are now nearing exhaustion.

This may be the time to consider factoring your debts, simply in order to get a proportion of the money owed to you into the bank at an earlier date, although you should be aware that the net cost of this will be greater than the savings on overdraft interest.

There is now a premium on chasing customers for money and deferring payment of suppliers until the last possible moment. You may not be the flavour of the month by doing so, but it is your company's survival that is at stake.

You should certainly reconsider your stock control and material purchasing arrangements. Lower your reorder points, reduce your buffer stocks, even at the risk of some stock-outs, and order only what you need for immediate production. Can you find material suppliers who will supply you on a 'Just-in-Time' basis?

What you should understand is that by reducing your working capital in this way you are not going to make any difference to your current asset value. All of the resulting movements in your balance sheet are going to be confined to the items that make up net current assets. What you squeeze out of working capital will simply have enabled you to avoid increasing your overdraft by an equivalent amount and, because your overdraft is also a part of your net current assets, the net result is a zero change. Also, because there is a limit to how far you can go in reducing debtors and stock and extending your trade creditors, this does tend to be only a once-off opportunity.

Apart from saving a little in interest charges, what you will have done—and this is the important aspect—is that you will have postponed for a month, or maybe two or three, the point at which you next need to face the bank manager. By that time you may well have better news to report.

Utilization of Tax Losses

This is where you really can benefit from creative accounting. The present rate of corporation tax is either 35 per cent or 25 per cent depending on the level of profit. Just suppose, for example, that your accumulated tax losses were £1 million and that another company with profits of more than that could legally acquire your tax loss. The result would be that it would reduce its tax liability by 35 per cent of £1 million, i.e. by £350 000, in the current financial year. They are clearly not going to pay you, however indirectly, all of that £350 000. You may split the difference in some way.

Let me give you a purely hypothetical example. Just suppose for a minute that you value the business as a going concern at a nominal £1000 and you value the tax loss at £350 000. Then suppose you sell out to another company for £351 000 and immediately arrange a management buy-out for £176 000, forming a new company in the process, but retaining your previous company name. You would immediately have new assets of £175 000, less some solicitors' charges. The other company has paid you £175 000 for tax losses of £1 million which will reduce their year-end tax bill by £350 000.

To do it legally is not nearly as straightforward as that, but a first-rate commercial lawyer may be able to find an opportunity for you which could be worth exploring further.

MAKING PROVISIONS

In Chapter 1 I recommended making provisions in the accounts for termination of any dead-wood management you found on arrival at the company. There are many other provisions you would be well advised to make at this point in order to give you the benefit of as clean a start as possible.

But whether you can afford to do this will depend on just how bad the present balance sheet really is. If you find yourself close to the point where the funds are running out, you should postpone this action until a later date. Any further provisions you make at this stage are simply going to reduce still further your asset value and so make it yet more difficult to secure any topping up of funds in the immediate future. It could actually reduce rather than extend the time-scale available to you.

On the other hand, if you are part of a larger group, or if you have a healthy balance sheet, then you should not hesitate to make as many provisions as you can. This may be one way of preventing the time-scale closing in on you later on.

Apart from providing for terminations, you should be thinking also of the following:

- How much redundant or slow-moving stock is there? You should make a provision for at least that part which you feel may never get used for production.
- Is there an adequate provision for bad debts? Any debt that is overdue is potentially a bad debt and you must make some provision for this.
- Are there any doubtful capitalizations, such as research and development expenditure, which have hitherto been capitalized in order to increase profit or reduce the losses? This may be the time to write this off, although you may be required to justify such a change in accounting convention.

- Is there a possibility of having to spend money restructuring the company before you get it turned round? If there is the remotest possibility of this, then make a provision right now.
- Check out in detail the pre-payments and accruals. Write off any pre-payments you possibly can, such as annual subscriptions. Make sure that there are no possible accruals that have been overlooked.

You should have no difficulty in persuading your auditors to agree to such provisions. They have a vested interest in presenting as conservative as possible a picture of your company's net worth. If you go to extremes in doing this, it may rebound on you in future years when you may find yourself making a profit and do not want it understated as a result of unrealistic provisions agreed in the past.

What you should be aiming to do right now is to get as much in the way of provisions as you possibly can written off against the previous month's accounts, or better still, the previous year's accounts. If you are new to the job, then the past is something you cannot be held accountable for, but from now on what happens is your responsibility.

It is prudent to avoid being in the position where the errors of the past can deliver a damaging impact on future accounts. That is what would happen, for example, if you had to fire some old staff and had no provision to do so, if you later had to scrap old stock, if old debts had to be written off or if you encountered large restructuring costs. These are not your fault and you must immediately ensure that they are consigned to the past in the form of adequate provisions in the accounts.

You could try to convince the auditors that the company must be relaunched on the market-place as part of the strategy for recovery, and that you need to make some provision for this as well. Be creative and you should find other potential provisions. At worst, the answer can only be no. You have nothing to lose and everything to gain by trying.

In the next chapter we shall address the survival plan. There may be action needed that will involve expense over and above the normal monthly outgoings. It helps at that stage if there have been provisions put aside that will limit the effect of such expenditure on the on-going accounts.

6

The survival plan

The survival plan should follow quickly from the initial situation appraisal and will be based on the understanding gained from that appraisal. The objective of this plan is to initiate fairly immediate action which will improve the company's results in the short term.

BASIC ELEMENTS OF THE PLAN

The basic elements of the survival plan will be to:

- Increase sales
- Reduce costs
- Secure necessary funding

We have already covered the question of funding in some detail in the previous chapter, when we examined the relationship between funding and time-scale at your disposal. The survival plan itself will be a means of selling the proposition that additional funding should be provided. It must convince the bank manager, the shareholders or whoever is going to provide the funds.

In this chapter we shall consider the way in which this plan should be prepared. We shall concentrate on ways and means of improving the performance of the business in the short term. The steps we shall now consider in more detail are these:

- Orientation to the problem
- The planning method

- The formal plan
- Implementation and project management

ORIENTATION TO THE PROBLEM

At the end of Chapter 4 we identified how the business performance could be improved:

- Increase sales towards break-even
- Reduce the break-even point.

If you recap on the ways of lowering the break-even point, you will
notice that all the possible courses of action for improving the
business performance can be distilled into two basic component
parts: sales and costs. Sales are necessary and desirable; costs,
however necessary, are to be avoided whenever possible.

Your best chance of survival in the difficult period ahead will be
if you are, or become, a sales-oriented company and regard 'costs'
as an all-embracing concept that includes material costs, the costs
of production and all the overheads, including the costs incurred
in selling.

An expert in the business of sales training has used a very
simple exercise for over 20 years to get his pupils properly
oriented. He shows them how important the sales function is in a
company by comparing it to the point of an arrow. He draws the
point and labels it 'sales'. He then draws in the shaft and the
flights, divides these up into compartments and invites his pupils
to name all the functions within their companies that impact on
their ability to get an order and give service to the customer.

As each function or department of the company is named, he
labels a compartment accordingly. He explains how the point of
the arrow, the sales function, is the part that makes the kill, and
that the shaft and flights are necessary only to support the point
en route to its target. The lesson is crystal clear. Everything apart
from the sales function is both a support function and a cost. It is a
very good model for a loss-making company to follow during the
survival phase.

THE PLANNING METHOD

The most important step in the planning method will be to:

● Identify possible action plans.

In selecting which action plans will together form the survival plan, they will be considered and short-listed taking account of:

● Lead-time of removing barriers to sales
● Constraints of time-scale and funding
● Cost–benefit analysis
● Probability of success
● Availability of management effort

Identify the Possible Action Plans

To identify these action plans needs an understanding of the present strengths and weaknesses of the company, including those of the sales team itself. What is really needed is a short-list of key actions which, if tackled successfully, will have the greatest possible impact on the bottom-line results as quickly as possible.

You will be at an advantage in doing this if you are able quickly to 'eyeball' the wider scene and home in on the really significant areas to address. Even if you are able to do this, it is still wise to involve others in this task, such as the management team and any external advisers who may be available to you.

The possible action plans you identify will be unique to your particular company situation, but there are some key areas where you should be looking for improvements; we shall consider in turn both of the performance-related elements of the survival plan which were stated at the beginning of this chapter:

● Cost reductions
● Increase in sales

There may be reasons why one or other of these should be the higher priority. We shall then look more closely at:

● Where to focus the action

COST REDUCTIONS

Cost reduction may be found in each of the three cost categories reported in the management accounts (see Table 3.1, page 26):

- Overhead costs
- Direct labour costs
- Material costs

Overhead costs

In the case of the XYZ Company (Table 3.1, page 26) overhead costs were by far and away the most significant cost category and that is often where the majority of savings can be made in the short run. Here is a short-list of how savings can be made:

- Challenge every controllable item of cost.
- Eliminate expenditure not producing results.
- Defer any expenditure that can be deferred.
- Set strict levels of authority.
- Keep personal expenses under tight control.
- Seek reductions in staff.

Challenge controllable costs   To supplement the management accounts we used in Chapter 3, you will need a detailed break-down of the individual items that are included under each of the three main overhead costs shown on the accounts. Make sure each item is then subdivided into controllable costs and uncontrollable costs. Rent and rates, for example, are uncontrollable; there is nothing you can do in the short term to reduce them. Travel and entertainment, on the other hand, are very definitely controllable.

List the controllable costs in descending order by value. Challenge each and every item with whoever spends the money and start pruning them one by one.

Eliminate costs not producing results   Are there any costs being incurred which are not going to yield a tangible benefit in the short term? If the answer is yes, then stop spending the money.

For example, expenditure on public relations could fall into that category in many companies. Any benefit accruing in the short term may be due to expenditure incurred several months ago. The on-going expense may not yield results for many months into the future. If that type of expenditure does have medium- to long-term benefits, then you can always include it in the budget again when you have nursed the company back to a healthier position.

Defer any expenditure that can be deferred Any expenditure that can be postponed should be. The easiest decision to make is to defer expenditure on replacement of company cars, vans or lorries, and on any other item that is due for replacement on a regular basis.

Set strict levels of authority You should set strict levels of authority regarding future expenditure. Any expense exceeding a certain amount must have your prior authorization. This gives you the chance to make sure that your staff are not spending needlessly and it also lets you challenge whether or not they have taken the time and trouble to get the best price. You may have to look carefully at all standing contracts (cleaning services, for example) just to verify that they are cost-effective.

Keep personal expenses under tight control You may have to be mean for a long time to come. Make the salesforce tighten their belts and stay in cheaper hotels. How many customers will notice if they are not wined and dined for a few months?

Seek staff reductions Add up the head-count. How many of the overhead staff can be saved without bringing the business to a halt? Most of your managers are going to defend the jobs in their departments, but ask them to list all the tasks each member of staff does and how long they spend on each task in the course of a month. They will have to distinguish between daily, weekly and monthly tasks in doing this.

You should find that quite a few of them are underemployed.

They may not appear to be, but that is because they are obeying Parkinson's First Law: that work expands to fill the time available for its completion. Perhaps you can combine two or three jobs or departments into one and make people savings as a result.

These are only some of the possibilities open to you. One thing however is not advisable, and that is to skimp on the maintenance of plant, equipment and buildings. That is often one of the least predictable elements of cost and it can be tempting to leave repairs for a month or two to defer expense. The danger is that if you do this, you may put your product quality and your productivity at risk, and possibly also the safety of your employees. People learn by example, and if they see broken machines or leaking roofs, they are quite likely to pay less attention to good housekeeping themselves.

Direct labour costs

Reductions in direct labour costs can come from:

- Reductions in the head-count
- Reductions in overtime working
- Improvements in methods
- Improvements in quality

Reductions in head-count   Are you working at less than full capacity? If so, how many people on the shopfloor can you save? In Chapter 4, when we looked at the effect of capacity utilization on the break-even calculation, we noted the pros and cons of this action. Remember that if you need an increase in sales as well as a reduction in costs before you break even, then you may need some or all of the surplus staff. You have to exercise fine judgement on that point.

Reductions in overtime   What you can and must do is to look at the cost of overtime working. Get the total wages bill split out between basic wages and overtime. Be careful that what is placed in front of you as overtime cost is really the total cost of the overtime hours worked, not just the overtime premium element of these hours, which is what your accountant may well give you unless you are quite specific.

Overtime working is habit-forming. People get used to it, especially where rates of pay are poor. If you are working at less than full capacity, you should consider a total freeze on overtime working or, failing that, a rigid upper limit that may not be exceeded without your approval.

An easy way to identify exactly who it is that clocks up all the overtime hours is to get a listing of the P60 earnings as of the last 5 April, with basic salary or the annual equivalent of hourly rates for a normal working week recorded alongside. You will learn a great deal from that simple exercise and you may find that a large part of your overtime cost is not confined to direct labour, but that you have to take action among the overhead staff as well.

Improvements in methods   What can be done to find the least-cost production routes? In most companies there will be significant scope for improvement. Are there any low-cost investments that could yield cost reductions? Do not rule these out just because money is tight. There may be a fairly spectacular payback, especially if the company has been too shortsighted in its approach to investment in the past.

Improvements in quality   The cost of poor quality is often not appreciated and the cost savings that accrue from improvements in quality can be very large indeed. If reject rates are running at 10 per cent, for example, and you reduce that to 3 per cent, then you will have reduced the direct labour unit cost by 7 per cent, and you will also have increased your useable production capacity by the same amount. Quality is a subject you should read about in much more detail.

Material costs

Reductions in material costs may be less easy to achieve so quickly, but you should consider the following:

- Price reductions
- Change to lower-cost materials
- Improvements in quality

Price reductions   Trying to get price reductions from suppliers not only takes time, you also have to get the old stock out of the system before you reap the benefits. You may already have started ordering less at a time and you may find suppliers actually looking for price increases because you are taking smaller quantities.

Change to lower-cost materials   If there is nothing very special about the materials you use, can you find a cheaper substitute? Or can you replace the use of costly 'specials' by buying standard products instead?

Improvements in quality   The benefits already noted regarding direct labour costs apply equally to material costs.

INCREASE SALES

The second part of the performance equation is increasing sales or, more specifically, net sales revenue. This can be achieved in three ways:

- Increasing selling prices
- Reducing customer credit claims
- Increasing sales volume, i.e. getting more orders

Winning more orders may in turn depend on:

- Removing barriers to sales

Increase selling prices

The policy that rarely succeeds is that of simply raising selling prices to the level that would arithmetically bring about break-even at the present level of production. It takes no account of the real world outside the company.

An opportunity to raise prices may exist if some or all of the following are true:

- Present price levels are lower than competitors' prices or the market-price level.
- Product benefits or service levels are higher than the competitor's offer.
- Material costs and uncontrollable costs can be shown to have increased since the present price level was fixed.
- The customer end-product is not price-sensitive.
- Customers are sympathetic to your problem and value your product and/or service.
- Customers would face a high cost of changing to an alternative supplier.

On the other hand, raising prices would invite customer resistance and could lead to loss of sales in the following circumstances:

- The product is undifferentiated and/or already priced at market-price level.
- Product quality, delivery reliability or after-sales service is poor.
- The customer end-product is price-sensitive and any increase in cost prices would have to be absorbed within the customer's own margins.
- There is a wide choice of alternative suppliers.
- There was a fixed-price contract covering a forward period.

Even if the opportunity to raise the list price is limited, it may be possible to raise prices indirectly, and in a way that draws less attention, by:

- Increasing packing and carriage charges

- Reducing quantity discounts
- Increasing small quantity premiums
- Increasing minimum invoice value

Reduce customer credit claims

This may be achieved by improving quality. The spin-off benefit will be to raise the value to the customer of the product or service you supply; this may in turn support an increase in selling price or help win more business.

Increase sales volume

There is no simple formula for achieving increased sales. The key to it will be highly specific to your company, its products and the market-place. It will be necessary to examine all of the following factors to identify where the weaknesses lie and to decide how these defects can be corrected:

- The competence of sales management. What is important is how the sales activity is directed and controlled.
- The capabilities of the sales team. The most successful will be those who understand and sell product benefits. The need for sales training must be considered.
- The level of resources used, both in field selling and in the sales office. Too high a resource level wastes money; too low a level will inhibit results.
- Sales pricing policy. Too many of the sales team offer this as the reason for lack of orders. Very often it is not the real reason. Be very critical and, if possible, talk to major customers yourself before you accept a need to reduce prices.
- How awareness is created in the market and how sales leads can be identified quickly and easily. This will depend on what back-up there is in the form of publicity and promotion, as well as the back-up given by the sales office to the salesforce.

- The level of customer service being provided. This will include response to enquiries as well as quality, delivery and after-sales service.

Remove Barriers to Sales

A prerequisite to increasing sales may be the removal of barriers to sales. This is very often the case in loss-making companies, especially where the record of the recent past is one of declining sales. It may well be that sales are falling through lack of sales effort, but a much more likely cause will be that the customers are voting with their feet for some reason. In this situation you should visit as many key customers as you possibly can and find out face-to-face what the reason for this is.

The main barriers to sales, but not necessarily in this order of importance, are these:

- Slow response to enquiries
- High price
- Poor quality performance
- Unreliable delivery performance

You can do something about price right away, but you must bear in mind the implication of marginal pricing; this was demonstrated in Chapter 4. Price reductions may bring short-term benefit, but will raise the break-even point.

It should be possible to find ways of speeding up the response to sales enquiries. If the process of cost estimating and quotation is not done by computer, it may be relatively simple to improve the system by building the estimating logic on a spreadsheet or by using a database language to do so.

If the problem is bad quality or unreliable delivery performance, there is a much more deep-seated problem to attend to and it may take much longer to correct. This may have a major impact on the shape of the survival plan and we must take account of that later in this chapter.

Where to Focus the Action

In deciding whether the main focus of action should be on cost reduction, increasing sales or removing barriers to sales, you should be guided by your sales trend or, better still, if the information is available, by the trend in your market share. Is this rising, is it static or is it declining?

- Rising sales: If you are reasonably sure that this trend will continue, then focus on cost reductions rather than trying to accelerate sales growth immediately. If market share is increasing, competitors will be reluctant to let this go on unchecked and you may need a healthier financial position to defend against their counter-attack. With growing sales you must also ensure that production capacity will support that growing order book.

- Static sales: the main focus should be on action plans to increase sales. Any reductions in costs will support these sales action plans by reducing the break-even point, so giving your sales manager a more attainable goal to reach.

- Declining sales: concentrate on removing barriers to sales in the first instance, with action plans for increasing sales following as a second stage. We shall consider shortly the timing aspects of that.

List the Possible Action Plans

Now that the possible action plans have been identified, list them on a sheet of paper under the following four headings:

Action   Benefit   Cost   Time

The benefit is the best estimate of the net monthly impact on the bottom line. In the case of additional sales, this is not the additional sales revenue, but the additional gross margin. If you are presently working below full capacity, it will instead be the additional added value until such time as full capacity is reached. The additional gross margin or added value will be offset by any on-going costs incurred as a result of this action.

Cost is the additional once-off cash outflow you will incur by taking this action. It does not include the value of the time of staff or any other resources you already employ and pay for. For the moment at least, it is academic whether this is revenue or capital expenditure; both involve a call on that scarce funding.

Under the heading time you should record how many months you believe it will take to achieve the benefits of the action. Be very careful when dealing with increases in sales. You must understand clearly the typical enquiry-to-order lead-time prevailing in the markets you serve and whether or not 'spot' business may be available. Unless there is a possibility of spot business, there will be an offset in time from launching the action plan to it bringing results. This will be equal to the typical enquiry-order lead-time.

Lead-time of Removing Barriers to Sales

When the key action is removing barriers to sales, to be followed by a second stage of increasing sales, then the relative timing of the two stages becomes important and is related to the typical enquiry-to-order lead-time.

It would be wrong to go all out and win new customers immediately, because in the present situation there would be a high chance of losing them after the bad experience they are likely to have with their first order. But do not assume that the barriers to sales must be dismantled *before* additional sales are sought.

Suppose the enquiry–order lead-time is nine months and that with really concerted action you could bring quality and delivery performance back to an acceptable level within five months. If you launch your second-stage action plan immediately, the main impact on your order intake will not occur until four months after you have become capable of providing a much higher level of customer service. On the other hand, if you wait until stage one is successfully completed, then you are postponing the benefit of any sales increase until 14 months into the future.

With a two-stage plan like this you must calculate exactly when to launch the second-stage plans, taking account of the relative time needed for both stages. If your new sales order lead-time is a lengthy one, you may have to take the gamble and launch your sales action plans before you can be sure that you have succeeded in dismantling the barriers to sales. On the other hand, in a spot business situation you would clearly divide them into two separate and consecutive stages.

Constraints of Time-scale and Funding

Remember also that you are working within the dual constraints of time-scale and availability of funds we examined in Chapter 5. Any action that will need more funds than you have access to is not viable for the moment. Any action that will not yield the benefit within the appropriate time-scale is not going to solve your short-term problem. That may not be a valid reason for postponing the action, especially if the medium-term benefit would be considerable, but right now you need to home in on the action that will produce benefit within the right time-scale.

Cost–Benefit Analysis

You can now rank that list of possible action plans by doing a simple cost–benefit analysis. The benefits will continue to accrue for months or perhaps years to come. For the moment you should ignore the benefits that will accrue beyond the immediate time-scale you are wrestling with. You are concerned only with short-term benefits in your fight for survival, so do not look beyond the month we identified in Chapter 5 as being that point where time runs out.

Let us suppose you have five months before the clock stops. That was the problem we looked at in Chapter 5. Let us also suppose that you have six possible action plans; in real life you will find many times that number, but we can limit it here to make this presentation a little simpler. Using the headings already suggested, the list might look like this:

Action plan	Benefit £	Cost £	Time (months)
1	2 700	1 500	3
2	1 000	2 000	2
3	4 000	2 000	4
4	300	0	1
5	6 000	10 000	5
6	500	300	2

In a healthy business all of these action plans would be worth implementing immediately, and even in your predicament they will all be worth attention sooner or later. The questions now are: which of them address the immediate time-scale? and what is the pecking order? The answers are not immediately obvious, so we need to list them again and this time we shall prepare a cash-flow analysis running out as far as the fifth period from now. In each case we shall assume that the cost is incurred up-front in month 1.

Action plan	Cumulative £ cash flow at future periods: 1	2	3	4	5
1	(1 500)	(1 500)	1 200	3 900	6 600
2	(2 000)	(1 000)	0	1 000	2 000
3	(2 000)	(2 000)	(2 000)	2 000	4 000
4	0	300	600	900	1 200
5	(10 000)	(10 000)	(10 000)	(10 000)	(4 000)
6	(300)	200	700	1 200	1 700

You will see that you can now rank these action plans in the following order: 1 3 2 6 4. Action plan 5, however attractive it may be in the longer term, does satisfy the constraint of time-scale.

This is a somewhat different view of cost–benefit analysis than will be found in the usual textbooks on the subject. There you will be shown how to rank these plans in terms of the rate of return over the future life of the investment, using techniques like discounted cash flow. This will become very important when you get the company out of danger and start planning for the future, but at this critical stage the future stops at month 5 unless you produce the action. This is all that matters.

The Probability of Success

You cannot be absolutely certain that all of these action plans will work, so you should make allowance for this. The best way is to 'guesstimate' the probability of success. You could include this as a fifth column on the cost–benefit analysis, and when you make your cost–benefit analysis you should then discount the monthly benefit accordingly. For example, if you felt that action 1 had only a 70 per cent chance of succeeding, then you would value the monthly benefits as only £1890 and not £2700. This helps give an added degree of realism to the decision-making process.

The biggest danger at this stage is over-optimism. You can usually quantify the cost of taking action fairly precisely, but benefits on the other hand tend to be overestimated rather than underestimated. It is surprising just how often it takes much longer to make it happen than was first thought. This is particularly true in the case of new sales orders.

When facing the issue of survival, over-optimism in these respects will do no good at all. If the benefits have not started accruing by the time you predicted, then the bank manager or shareholders may simply take the view that they are not likely to do so at all, even though your own signposts are indicating the opposite.

There will be some action plans on the list that perhaps you cannot quantify in terms of benefit. For example, you may need to replace your production manager in order to address major problems in the works. The benefit of this may be less tangible than the other action plans on the list, and you may need to do a 'sore-thumbing' exercise to slot such action plans into the pecking order.

Availability of Management Effort

You must consider carefully how you are going to go about implementing the selected action plans. Do not forget that you still have to manage the business from day to day and this absorbs part of your time. Your managers are in the same position and day-to-day business will account for a greater part of their working day than it will of your own. Both you and your managers, therefore, have a limited amount of time to devote to the management of change.

If you tackle too many different action plans at one and the same time, you may end up dissipating the available effort in so many directions that none of them gets tackled effectively. On the other hand, there may be some action plans that can quite simply be slotted into the day-to-day tasks of managing the business, such as a simple change of sales pricing policy. The major action plans, however, are likely to need a fair amount of effort and, probably, effort on the part of a number of different people in the organization.

Only you can decide just how much change you can tackle at once without the day-by-day business grinding to a halt. But it has to add up in benefit terms to be sufficient to address your problem of time-scale. You have to make a selection from that short-list and these together will comprise your survival plan.

THE FORMAL PLAN

The survival plan should be a formal document and it should have the following contents:

- A revised forecast for the periods ahead, which will be supported by:
  - A recap of the short-range forecast you made in Chapter 3, and
  - A tabulation of the changes that will be made to that forecast as a result of this survival plan.
- The cash-flow forecast for these periods.

- A statement of how much additional funding is needed and when it will be needed.
- A written summary of all the selected action plans, specifying the action itself, costs and benefits, time-scale, who will be responsible for implementation and how and when it can be judged to have succeeded or not.

This is not just a paper exercise. It will serve two very important purposes:

- It will give the plans the status needed for action to happen. By getting it down in writing, and by circulating it to your managers, you are giving it a status it would not have if it was just talked about. It is less likely to be overlooked or just be given lip-service.
- It is a selling document. When you give a copy to the bank manager or shareholders you are giving them a selling document. You are selling them the improvements in performance that you yourself are going to bring about in the short run, and this will help persuade them to grant the funding you need.

IMPLEMENTATION AND PROJECT MANAGEMENT

Implementing this survival plan successfully requires single-mindedness of purpose. You must focus people's minds 100 per cent on these action plans, as they are the key to survival. This can most easily be achieved by good project management:

- Give each of the action plans the status of a major project.
- Manage them as major projects.
- Allocate resources to them.
- Monitor progress constantly.
- At management meetings review each plan as a separate item on the agenda.
- Make sure that everyone in the company knows that these projects are in hand and that they know why they are being carried out. Keep everyone updated as to the progress and results that have been attained.

7

A period of intensive care

The survival plan will by now have been approved and you will have begun the key task of implementing the various action plans. This is a critical phase in the life of the company. Until the benefits of the action plans are attained, and the company begins to move towards financial stability, you must look upon this company as if it were a patient under your intensive care.

You will take the pulse from minute to minute. You will check to ensure that the bleeding has been staunched and, if necessary, you will give a blood transfusion. In this case the life-blood is the cash flow and the transfusion is the additional funding you have been able to secure. The pulse is the day-by-day progress of the company, a vital part of which will now be the progress that is being made towards successful implementation of the action plans for survival.

KEEPING A FINGER ON THE PULSE

Throughout this critical period you must have your finger on the pulse all of the time. In this chapter we shall consider the ways in which you should do this:

- Monitor progress of action plans.
- Set up reporting systems.
- Set targets.
- Communicate targets and achievements.
- Key performance indicators.

We shall then look beyond the survival stage and begin preparing for the recovery phase. When planning the strategy for recovery we shall need good data relating to product profitability. The key to this will be:

- The product costing system

Monitor Progress of Action Plans

If any action plan is drifting off course, you will direct it back on course. If a particular plan looks like being stillborn, you should abort it before you waste too much valuable time and money. If a better action plan presents itself, you may decide to add it to the programme.

You should not be too proud to alter course if you have to; after all, there was very limited time and information available when the survival plan was being prepared, and it will be understandable if you did not get it exactly right the first time. Each day that passes will be bringing a deeper insight into the problems and possible solutions and it is only right that you should react to this.

On the other hand, take care that you do not prejudice the chances of survival by making too many or too frequent changes to the plans. Above all, avoid making a complete U-turn; that will only confuse your staff and lower your credibility with them just when you can least afford it.

Reporting Systems

In addition to monitoring the progress of the action plans, you will need a simple but effective means of monitoring the health and progress of the business as a whole. You need to be as fully informed as possible and you cannot afford to wait until the month-end management accounts and balance sheet are prepared.

Too much happens, even in the brief space of a month, that you need to know about much more immediately. You can ensure this by setting up key reporting systems, which will provide information on a daily or weekly basis. This key reporting should cover the following:

- New order bookings
- Production output
- Sales despatches
- Scrap or reject levels
- Customer credit claims
- Staff attendance and overtime working
- Financial commitments made, e.g. orders placed for stock or production materials or for overhead expenditure
- The cash position

There may be others that will be relevant to the particular problems of your own company.

Set Targets

If you take a step back at this stage, you will realize that even this is only recording what *has* happened. Would it not be better if you first made everyone in the company aware of what *should* be happening?

You can do this by setting targets, at the start of each period, that are consistent with the current short-range forecast. You should set daily and/or weekly targets for each of the items within the scope of the reporting systems you set up. You will then be in a position to compare the cumulative achievement compared to target as each day of the month passes.

It may be prudent to set these targets a little higher than is actually needed to achieve the forecast. In other words, add a contingency allowance.

Communicate Targets and Achievement

Better still, display these targets and the actual achievements on a large display chart in the office and on the shopfloor so that everyone in the company knows what they need to achieve and how successful they have been.

Most people put in a fair day's work for the money they are paid, but very few will be able to measure the success of that work unless you tell them. The majority of the employees will, in fact, be very concerned about the success of the business; it is their future job security that is at stake, just as much as your own.

Nothing will be more demotivating to them than allowing the days to pass by without comment and then informing them at the end of the month that they have fallen short of target. You may well think in a time-frame of a month because that is the conventional accounting period, but most of your staff will think in a time-frame of just one day. You will have a very much higher chance of success if you report back to them their achievement, or their shortfall, within *their* time-frame, i.e. on a daily basis.

Key Performance Indicators

Come the month-end, when the management accounts and balance sheet are available, you will then pause and put the month in perspective. You will analyse each and every item on the accounts and you will again look a few months into the future and revise your short-range forecasts, hopefully in an upwards direction now that the benefits from the action plans are beginning to bear fruit.

Table 7.1   Key performance indicators

1	Order bookings:	home	£K
		export	£K
		total	£K
		number of orders	
2	Number of sales enquiries		
	Number of new orders		
	Conversion ratio		%
3	Order book:	*total*	£K
		overdue	£K
4	Shipments:	home	£K
		export	£K
		total	£K
		number of invoices	

Table 7.1   *Continued.*

5	Production value: factory 1		£K
		factory 2	£K
		total	£K
6	Production value per direct hour:		
		factory 1	£
		factory 2	£
		total	£
7	Material costs:	metal	%
		plastic	%
		total	%
8	Direct and works costs		£K
	Sales and distribution costs		£K
	Finance and admin. costs		£K
9	Debtors		mths
	Stocks:	raw material	mths
		total	mths
10	Number of employees		
	Absentee level		%
	Overtime level		%
11	Number of credit notes		
	Customer returns		£
12	Rejections:	quantity, factory 1	%
		quantity, factory 2	%
		value, factory 1	%
		value, factory 2	%
13	Delivery performance:		
		on time	%
		<1 week late	%
		1–2 weeks late	%
		2–4 weeks late	%
		>4 weeks late	%
14	Order shipment shortfall		%
15	Production forecast: month + 1		£K
		month + 2	£K

But it helps put things in perspective for your management team to manage the business if you can find a way to help them focus on the most important elements of performance. The easiest way to do this is to present a set of key performance indicators.

These key performance indicators should be presented on a single sheet of paper, as in Table 7.1. This is an example that was highly specific to a particular situation and set of problems. Some items include budget and actual figures for both current month and year-to-date; others are limited to current month only. Against each item is shown the unit of measurement. It is important that there be a set of unambiguous definitions so that everyone knows and understands exactly how each item is calculated or measured.

You must stop and think just what elements of performance are key to managing your own business, especially during the critical survival stage. There is no standard format that can be guaranteed to apply to a specific situation, so you should concentrate on the major problem areas of the business when composing this reporting document.

In the company shown in Table 7.1 the production was split between two factories and it was vital to see some elements of performance in the context of the specific factory. This may not be true in your case, but there will be some other items of major importance, which you may need to include instead. For example, you may choose to split order bookings, production and shipments by product group.

Once the system for producing this report is established, you may consider producing an abridged version of this key document on a weekly basis as well so as to help drive the business in the right direction on an even more immediate basis.

When you assemble your management team together, this is the document you should review with them, rather than the formal accounts documents. It will focus attention on the key items of performance and it will help identify those that need special attention or correction over the next period.

THE PRODUCT COSTING SYSTEM

Very soon we shall begin to prepare a strategy for recovery. Understanding product profitability will be very important when we do so. This information will come from a product costing system, so now is the time to ensure that there is such a system which will produce reliable and useful information when it is needed. To be useful product costing data need only be *approximately* correct; very often trying to make it perfect also makes it wrong.

We shall consider both situations you may find in this company:

- A system already exists: challenge the basis of it.
- There is no system: how to set it up.

Challenge the Existing Costing System

There may already be a product costing system in the company. If there is, then challenge it in some depth to make sure it is soundly based. There are two important questions to be asked:

- How is overhead recovery treated?
- Is the system based on actual or standard costs?

Treatment of overhead recovery

A costing system that attributes general overhead costs to the product costs will present misleading information. This may be difficult for your accounts staff to accept, they may believe it necessary to have a system in which the total of the product costs add up to the total of the company costs.

Remember the basic arithmetic we saw when studying the break-even point in Chapter 4. Getting the results right is all about generating enough gross margin to recover the overhead costs of the business. What you really need to know from a costing system is what gross margin and added value are generated by each product. The definition of these is totally clear from the

management accounts format, which was selected in Chapter 3.
Overhead costs do not enter into the calculation of either added
value or gross margin.

If the existing system draws overhead costs into the product
costing system, find out how to eliminate these. If the reports
show overhead recovery as a separate item, this will be easy, but if
it is done by adding an element of overhead recovery into the
direct labour rates, it may be more difficult. Is it possible to
amend direct labour rates to exclude overhead recovery and can
the historic data then be reprocessed to use these revised rates
instead?

Actual costs vs. standard costs

Next check whether the costing system is based on actual costs or
on standard costs. If it is based on standard costs, you will be
much better served by the data you have. But even so, spend some
time checking that the standards used are realistic. The critical
questions are these:

- Are the labour rates based on sound engineering time
  standards?
- Is the work actually being done the way the standard costing
  assumes that it is being done?
- Have any changes been made to the bills of materials since the
  standard was established?

If you have an actual costing system, then the accuracy or
inaccuracy of this will be totally dependent on how good or bad
the recording is that takes place in the stores and on the shopfloor.
The variable quality of data recording will often produce a wide
variance in the apparent costs of the same product from one works
order to the next.

Before you use actual cost data to establish product profitability it will be necessary to have this information from as many
production periods or as many works orders as possible. Then you
should 'sore-thumb' out any abnormal data at the extremes of the

range before striking an average for that product. That way you will rid yourself of the worst of the inaccuracies that result from this costing method.

How to Get Standard Costs Easily

If there is no costing system at present, then setting one up must now be a high priority. You should bear in mind that the data only need to be approximately correct. An actual costing system is more than likely to give figures that are perfect, but wrong.

The best data will be based on standard costs, but ones that are then modified to take account of the reality of the situation. This need not be a difficult task. It all depends on just how many discrete products are produced. If there is a limited number of products, it will be easy, but if you are in a jobbing-shop type of business, it might be much more laborious.

We shall consider first the existing systems from which standard costs can easily be derived. Both of the following should contain all or most of the information needed to produce standard product costs:

- Works production documentation
- Product cost estimates

In considering these we must test the validity of the information. Then finally we must consider some shortcuts and approximations that can be made, both to keep the system as simple as possible and also to reflect the real-life situation as opposed to the theoretical or standard.

Works Production Documentation

This tells the shopfloor how to make the product. It should comprise:

- Bill of materials
- Job instructions

If there is no works documentation, it begs the question how the shopfloor are expected to make the product correctly. You should begin by getting proper works documentation established; that may take some time. Make sure the information goes into the computer and not just on pieces of paper. Provided it is on the computer you will later be able to use this as the basis for standard costs.

Where the documentation does exist a number of challenges must be made:

- Is the job still actually being made in this way?
- Have any changes been made to materials content?
- Does the job instruction sheet indicate the times allowed for each work element? If it does not, then there is now an urgent need to establish time standards.

If there is a limited number of work-stations, and not too much variation in work-rate depending on specific products, it may pay to get proper engineering time standards calculated by an industrial engineer, even if this means calling on external help.

Where the production routes are complex, or if there is a great deal of variety from one job to the next, you may need the end-results more quickly than such a task could be completed. In that case, imperfect as it may be, sit down with your production manager and construct some standards as realistically as possible on a broad-brush basis. This is not the ideal solution, but you have a problem of time-scale, so once again it is going to be necessary to be only approximately correct.

Cost Estimating Systems

Another possible basis for standard costs, especially in a jobbing type of business, may be the cost estimating system that was used to prepare the sales quotation. This will be valid provided that it was based on:

- An accurate bill of materials
- The proposed production route

- Realistic rates of work

To be useable the data must also still be available. Have the cost estimates been retained? Better still, have they been retained within the computer? If so, could they form the basis of standard costs?

If the cost estimate does not start from a bill of materials and a planned production route, then it has little validity. You may be losing money or business or both, because you are estimating costs incorrectly and are, therefore, arriving at an invalid basis for the quoted selling price.

In that case, can you build a simple spreadsheet to do the cost estimating? If you can, then each time a cost estimate is prepared this can be saved on disk; and when you get the order and go into production there will be standard costs already to hand.

These standards will, of course, only be valid if the job is made the same way it was presumed to be made at the estimating stage. If jobs are not being made in the same way as they were estimated, then you could still be losing money even if the job had originally been costed correctly. The only answer is to make the cost estimators and production planners work more closely and communicate better with each other.

Shortcuts and Approximations

There are some simple, but reasonably valid, shortcuts which can be made to reduce the amount of work involved in standard costing, but which will none the less lead to that approximately correct answer.

- Material costs. If you look at the total company spend on materials, you will most probably find that an 80/20 rule applies. Twenty per cent of the materials should account for 80 per cent of the material costs. In the system you set up it will be a reasonable approximation if you cost in detail only those key materials and then add on the appropriate uplift to take care of the remainder.

- Direct labour. The same applies to direct labour. It should be valid to apply an appropriate mark-up to recover the costs of the people who move work about or who issue materials from the stores. The same will apply to the costs of shopfloor supervision and other direct labour overheads, such as social security charges and pension contributions.

However you arrive at them, these standard costs will tell you only what the product cost *should* have been. That may be all very well in a healthy business, where you can devote part of your management effort towards corrective action by studying the variance analyses. In a loss-making situation it is more prudent to have a view of product profitability that takes account of most of the things that actually do go wrong.

Assuming that you have already taken account of variances due to changes in material prices or wage rates, then the two things that will account for most of the variance from standard are:

- Rejection levels
- Production efficiency

Simple approximations can be made to take account of these.

Rejection Levels

The easiest way to measure the true reject level is:

- Count the good production passing final inspection.
- Record how much of the key material was issued to the job. This key material issue can easily be converted to its equivalent units of finished production.
- The difference between the two figures will approximate to the overall rejection rate and can be expressed as a percentage. That information should be an integral part of the quality system. If it is not, then you should consider setting up on a personal computer a simple quality record system, product by product. This can be done with the help of a database language.

Production Efficiency

Measuring production efficiency is a little more difficult. To be of real use it should be done department by department. What makes this task complex is when you try to do it job by job. The simpler way is to measure total output over a period (a week, for example), and then spend half an hour each week working out approximately what the output should have been. You can then express efficiency as a percentage of standard and plot this on a graph to show the trends or the average achieved consistently over a much longer period.

Adjusting the Standard Costs

With these relatively simple data you can now turn the standard costs into approximate real costs. Using a spreadsheet you can apply a factor to all the direct labour costs to reflect the prevailing production efficiency in the different work-centres. Suppose that in one department efficiency was only 75 per cent of standard. You would then mark up that direct labour cost by 100/75.

Rejected work has had materials used on it and it has had labour expended on it. The last adjustment in the calculations should be to mark up both the material and direct labour costs to take account of the prevailing reject rates on that product. If the quality records show that the average reject rate for this product is 15 per cent, both material costs and direct labour costs must be marked up by 100/85, and in the case of direct labour this is applied in addition to the mark-up for production efficiency.

8

The move to firm ground

We must now assume that your survival plan has been successful and that the company has reached a more stable position from which you may now move forward from the survival stage to the recovery stage. You will have moved out of a quicksand and onto a position of firm ground; that is a significant milestone and one that deserves not to pass unnoticed.

Over recent months you will have begun a process of fact-finding and understanding. You now know a great deal more about the business than when you first started. In planning the strategy for longer-term recovery that fact-finding must now be done in a very systematic fashion; so we must now think in more detail about what information is needed and how you can go about procuring it.

STRATEGY

Before we do that, let me set the scene for this next stage by using a military analogy. By reaching firm ground you will have lived to fight another battle. That has a military sound to it. You are about to start thinking about your future strategy, and the whole concept of strategy and strategic planning, has its origins in the age-old game of warfare. You are in fact engaged in a form of warfare, but it is business warfare rather than military warfare.

The enemy are your competitors and the field of battle is the market-place you compete in. Your armies are your employees.

Your military hardware includes your plant and equipment, and your ammunition is your product range. Both warfare and business require adequate funding.

Stop for a moment and picture where you stand on the field of battle. When you took on this task of turning the company round you were in a similar position to the commander of a routed army, with its infantry battalions bogged down in a field of mud. All around you the competitors—the enemy—occupy the commanding heights. They, for the moment, have a strategic advantage over you.

You will not gain a position even of strategic parity until you too get your forces onto higher ground. If there is not enough high ground, you may need to dislodge the enemy and that may be a fairly bloody process.

Over the last few months all of your effort has been concentrated on getting the remains of your army out of the quagmire and onto firm ground. It did not matter what direction you moved in; firm ground is firm ground, whether you went forwards, backwards or sideways to reach it, but at least you are on it.

The next step is to reach one of the heights overlooking this battleground, from where you will have an advantage over any army on the plain of mud below you and from where you will be nearer to parity with the enemy on the opposing heights.

Let us suppose that from this position of firm ground you are facing north and that there is high ground on all four points of the compass. The enemy are entrenched on the high ground to the north, they have outposts to east and west, but the hills to the south are unoccupied. Which of these four hills are you going to try to occupy?

Von Clausewitz, one of the founders of strategic thinking, said, 'In strategy everything is very simple, but not very easy.' In this case the answer appears simple. But is it?

What happens if you take that apparently least-risk option of the hill to the south, only to find that it ends in a 1000-foot cliff-face to an angry sea below? You need the security of supply lines from the rear, as well as ground in the rear that you can retreat to if attacked. That cliff-face forecloses on both of these.

Would it make more sense to attempt to take the hills to west or east, especially if these were taking you closer to your strategic objective? Or even the occupied hill to the north if that were the way to link up again with severed lines of supply?

STRATEGIC DIRECTION

The decisions you will shortly have to make bear a close approximation to such a situation. The elements of choice remain the same as they were when you embarked on the survival plan. Recovery will depend on increasing sales and/or reducing costs. Increased sales may be sought from the same products and in the same markets as you have now, or you may consider new products or new markets. A large reduction in costs may be possible only if you contract, by withdrawing from some products and/or markets.

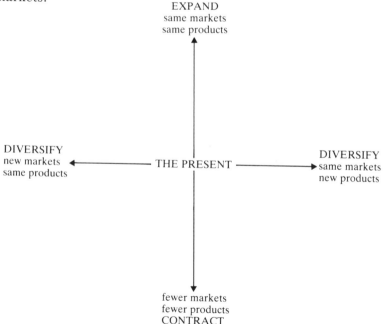

Figure 8.1   The strategic compass

Figure 8.1 shows these options plotted on the strategic compass. On or above the east–west axis represents growth; below it is contraction. The north–south axis represents no new markets or products; to either side lie new markets or new products.

These business options equate to the surrounding hills in that military example. You can go north; in this case it means that you are going to try to grow out of trouble. That is always a high-risk option. Just how big a risk remains to be seen when we know more about the market and your competitors and their products.

When the option of increasing sales of existing products within existing markets does not exist, or carries too high a risk, the other ways of achieving growth are to:

- Find new markets for the existing products.
- Find new products to supply to existing markets.

On the compass rose these are the hill-tops to the east and west.

The option of the hill to the south is very often the most sensible, but the most painful. It means restructuring the company by removing a sufficient part of its cost structure in order to create a viable business at a lower level of sales. We shall look in more detail at this process in Chapter 14.

Your options are not limited to the four points of the compass. By combining two of the adjacent cardinal options in varying degrees, you may take any compass heading that makes the greatest strategic sense. But beware of trying to combine east and west. Attacking a new market with a new product is the highest-risk option of all.

THE NEED TO REGAIN STRENGTH

Just as important as the strategic direction you take is what you do inside the company to redress its weaknesses and make it stronger. It needs that strength not only to protect it from attack during the long march to high ground. Once there it will have to defend itself against attack; and when the time is right you will need that strength to go onto the offensive.

For the moment we are not in a position to make the decision as to which hill-top to aim for and it is too important to be decided subjectively. We need much more information before planning the strategy for recovery. Not only that; the orientation recommended in Chapter 6, when the survival plan was being prepared, needs modification. At that stage we focused singlemindedly on only *sales* and *costs*. That focus must now be broadened out so that our thinking recognizes primarily the *market* and the *company*.

THE KEY QUESTIONS

The key to ultimate business success is when a company possesses all of the following advantages:

- A competitive market position
- An attractive market
- Effective routes to the market
- An effective internal organization

A competitive market position in turn depends on the company having:

- Competitive product benefits
- A competitive cost structure.

When we come to preparing the strategy for recovery, our thinking is going to be led by the answers to the questions: How competitive? How effective? How attractive? Over the next three chapters we shall consider what information is needed to answer these questions and where it can be obtained. We shall subdivide the information collection into three main subjects:

- The market (Chapter 9)
- The industry structure (Chapter 10)
- Your own company (Chapter 11)

9

Understand the market

Understanding the market is a key factor in formulating the strategy for recovery. Before gathering any information we must first answer the question:

- What business are you in?

The answer will define the business clearly in terms of market sectors. Then comes the task of:

- Market analysis

Most of this analysis will relate specifically to individual market sectors and the information we acquire will provide part of the answer to the question:

- How attractive is the market?

WHAT BUSINESS ARE YOU IN?

You must perceive your business in terms of the company's products and the markets for these products, and not in terms of the manufacturing processes used to make the products. Let us take an example.

Suppose the following description applied to the XYZ Company:

- Core manufacturing process: screen-printing
- Production materials: sheets of metal or plastic

- Products: nameplates and graphic display panels
- End-customer products: automotive, domestic appliance and consumer electronics products

What business is that company in? Many would describe it as being in the screen-printing business, but this company's business is actually making nameplates and graphic display panels for supply to the automotive, domestic appliance and consumer electronics markets.

It is very important that the business you are in is defined in terms of products and markets. Defining it the other way, e.g. in terms of the production process or production materials used, can lead to a number traps:

- A customer with no prior awareness of the company could misunderstand what product or service was being offered. In the example above, if one of the sales team described the company as being in the screen-printing business, a sales prospect could associate that with printed T-shirts, which are also screen-printed.
- You will behave as if the market was a moon revolving around your earth, or production process, when instead you should be reacting as if the company were an earth revolving around its sun, or market-place. You will expect the world to come rushing to buy whatever you can make as a result of the processes you have, when you should instead be asking what it is that you need to make in order to satisfy the changing needs of the market. That first way of thinking very often leads to a dead-end somewhere along the way.
- When you come to advertise you will choose the wrong media. In the example we took, those who see themselves as being in the screen-printing business will choose trade magazines relating to screen-printing rather than the media relating to the end-customers' products. Their advertising message is much more likely to be seen by competitors and not by customers.

Identify the Market Sectors

The market is therefore the combination of product and market. You may well make more than one product or supply more than one market, in which case you will have multiple product/ markets. Not only that, there may be some differentiation within these product/markets. One of the most common is the distinction between the high-volume, low-price end of the product/ market and the low-volume, high-price end.

The net result is that within your wider market there will be a number of distinct market sectors in which you compete, or may compete, for business. You may find that your customers or your competitors differ from one market sector to the next.

Much of the information you will set out to gather must therefore be related to these very specific market sectors. When we come to planning the strategy for recovery most of our thinking will be at this level of market sector.

THE MARKET ANALYSIS

The starting point in the gathering of information will be an analysis of the market and market sectors, partly in quantitative terms, and the purpose of this will be to answer the following key questions, most of which will have a bearing on how attractive or unattractive the market is:

- What is the size of the market?
- What is the growth rate?
- Are there identifiable market cycles?
- What is the life-cycle status?
- What drives the market?
- What is the natural geographical extent?

What Is the Size of the Market?

You need to know the size of the market to understand how big a part you play in it. Your own sales expressed as a percentage of the total size of the market will be your market share. The main implications of market size and market share are:

- The bigger the market you compete in, the more attractive that market will be for you.
- It is easier to achieve additional sales if market share is relatively low. The larger the market share, the more difficult it becomes to carve out a still bigger share, especially if there are competitors who also have significant market shares.

Market size can be expressed in terms of both volume and value. Volume represents the number of units of sales—the number of motor cars, for example, in the case of a car manufacturer. In the case of semi-finished materials, the yardstick is much more likely to be tonnes, gallons, square metres or whatever is the accepted unit of measurement within the industry.

In many cases it may not be appropriate to think in volume terms, or it may not be possible to locate statistics expressed this way, especially if the product is a component part, which is used on someone else's end-product. In that case you may have no option but to express the market size solely in terms of its value.

Sources of Information

Data relating to market size can be obtained from a number of sources:

- Trade associations. The easiest way will be if you belong to a trade association that collects member company sales statistics, collates them and then makes available the total market data to all the members. You may have to treat this information with caution and make some adjustments to take account of:
  - Important competitors who are not members.
  - Members whose sales include products you do not make.
- Government statistics. There may be a *Business Monitor* publication covering your products. To select the right one will

first involve identifying your products in the Index of Commodities. How to get this information is covered in more detail in Appendix 1 (see page 225). A major problem with Business Monitors is that they may relate only to fairly broad groups of products, and you may not be able to home in precisely on your own market.

- Suppliers. An easy way of getting market statistics might be to approach all the major suppliers to your industry to see if they have compiled this information for their own sales and marketing use.
- Your own estimates. If none of these other sources can provide the data you need, you may have to fall back on making your own estimates based on other sources of information. It may be necessary to estimate competitors' sales in order to quantify the market (this will be examined in Chapter 10).

If your market includes overseas countries, it may be more difficult to find market data. The most likely sources of this information will be:

- Your own branches or agents overseas, who should be familiar with the sources of information available in their countries.
- Department of Trade and Industry (see Appendix 1).

As with so much information, information about the market only needs to be approximate. An error of a few per cent either way is not going to make much difference to any interpretation you make.

It is important, however, to distinguish between what the industry produces and what the market consumes. This is particularly important if there is a high level of import penetration. We shall turn shortly to what the 'natural' geographic market is, but suppose for the moment that it is the whole of the United Kingdom. What the market consumes will be calculated as follows:

	UK production
plus	imports
minus	exports
equals	UK consumption

Many of the statistics readily available may relate only to UK production. The market may be significantly greater or less than that, depending on the relative flow of imports and exports. You may have to make allowance for this. If your trade association does not possess this information it may be obtained from the appropriate DTI *Business Monitor*.

What Is the Growth Rate?

It helps enormously in a turn-round situation if you have a growing market. It is easier to increase sales without having to take business from the competition. In a declining market everyone is going to be fighting just to stand still, so the odds of success are much less favourable.

The source of this information should be the same as the source used to establish the size of the market. By taking the same data, but for a collection of previous periods, you will establish the rate of growth, both period by period and in the longer term.

Are There Any Identifiable Market Cycles?

When looking at the growth rate you should not confine yourself to the recent past. It may be important to look further back to the major milestones in your industry or in the economy as a whole. In doing so, you will be looking for the ups and downs in the pattern of market growth.

Unless your market is a very new one, go back if you can to the oil crisis of 1974, and if you are in a very mature business then go back, if possible, to the end of the Korean War in 1952. These are two very important milestones in the international economy. The chances are that you will then find both shorter-term cyclical movements and a longer-term trend. Understanding these is extremely important.

What Is the Life-cycle Status?

The longer-term trend will tell you something about the life-cycle status of your market. Nothing lasts for ever. Technological change leads to product substitution. New products emerge and others decline.

The life-cycle of a product or service begins with a period of growth, often rising very steeply, after which it arrives at a plateau. Sometimes this may last for years or decades; sometimes it may be very brief. One day the decline will start and this can be very swift indeed.

Consider what happened to electromechanical accounting machines, for example. As recently as the early sixties this was a new and growing market. The product was a substitute for mental arithmetic and hand-written ledgers. The growth rate was so fast that it was not uncommon for sales territories to be divided into two every year. Within less than 20 years these machines had become museum pieces as microchip technology enabled first mini-computers and later personal computers to do more work at less cost.

The signs of terminal decline are relatively easy to read. When the long-term trend line projects forward to near zero, only false optimism can lead to its misinterpretation. What is more difficult to see in true perspective at the time is the early growth phase.

The great danger lies in believing that early growth will simply continue at the historical rate, but this is not so. The growth phase typically follows an S-shaped curve, and the levelling out of growth at the top of this curve is associated with the point at which a process of product substitution has run its course. This levelling out is preceded by the most rapid rate of growth and it is towards the end of this rapid growth phase that there is the greatest danger of misunderstanding future trends.

Very often the greatest additions to production capacity are made just before the growth flattens out. The result can be a market much more competitive, and therefore much less attractive, than it need have been if only the major players had understood more clearly the ultimate limits to growth.

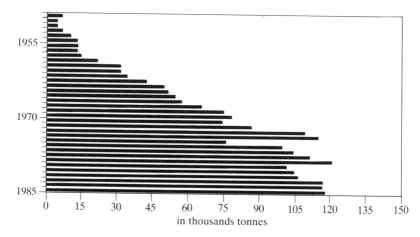

Figure 9.1   UK aluminium distribution market
Source: British Alcan Aluminium Plc

Case study—S-shaped growth curve   A good illustration of the S-shaped curve, and the failure to interpret it correctly, can be seen in the UK aluminium distribution market. The market growth over a 35-year period is shown in Fig. 9.1.

Although aluminium was discovered over 100 years ago, it remained expensive in relation to other materials until the need for aircraft alloys during the Second World War provided the stimulus to the larger-scale production and fabrication which made it a cost-effective substitute for other materials. As demand for the metal increased, an independent distribution industry grew with it to serve the customers who were too small to buy directly from the producers.

During the fifties and sixties many of these distributors became relatively large companies. By the early seventies this market had become visibly large in volume and was growing more rapidly than ever. This prompted the aluminium producers to integrate downstream and acquire previously independent distributors. Because UK entry to the European Community was on the horizon overseas producers as well as UK producers followed this course. Within a few years the producers owned just over half the industry and at once embarked on an expansion of the distribution facilities needed to secure them a higher share of what they saw as a growth market.

Figure 9.1 is a typical illustration of the S-shaped curve of the growth phase. Growth begins relatively slowly; in Fig. 9.1, this covers the period from the end of the Second World War to the mid-fifties. Then comes a period of rapid growth; in the figure this lasted until 1974. Finally, as the market matures, the growth slows down following the top of the letter S, and this is what has happened from the mid-seventies onwards.

In that particular industry the effect of this S-shaped growth pattern was not appreciated at the time. The major capacity additions in aluminium distribution were made *after* the growth had begun to flatten out. That flattening out of market growth was believed at the time to be a temporary phenomenon caused by the oil crises of 1974 and 1979.

It was not until the mid-eighties that it became fully appreciated that the real reason the growth curve had flattened was because the effective limits of product substitution had been reached. Meanwhile, the previous ten years' expansion of capacity had created an industry more cut-throat and less profitable than it need have been.

What Drives the Market?

From the analysis of trends you will have identified:

- Long-term trends
- Shorter-term cyclical trends

To understand these trends fully it is necessary to appreciate what is driving the market.

Long-term trends

The major factor underlying long-term trends will be the life-cycle status of the product. As we have seen this is driven by:

- Product substitution

Other factors that may explain long-term trends are:

- Underlying growth in the national or international economy.
- Political changes, which may open new markets or close existing markets. The liberalization of Eastern Europe in the nineties may be a particularly significant example of this.

The process of product substitution may take place at different levels in a manufacturing hierarchy:

- Raw materials
- Component parts
- Finished product

If your business is making raw materials or component parts, you may be affected not only by substitution of the product you supply, but also by the process of product substitution which takes place at the level of your customers' products.

In all instances of product substitution there is a limit which will be reached when the displaced product is no longer used. It would be wise also to be examining the market for that product to see how far it has declined from its peak and how much scope is left for further substitution.

With new consumer products like microwave ovens, the rapid growth rate of the early years will stop when a majority of households owns one. After that the market will become a replacement market, which will be much more static. The same will be true of many items of industrial machinery or plant.

Cyclical trends

Just as misleading as expecting the initial long-term growth to continue for ever upwards would be to project the prevailing trend foward from the middle of a cyclical upturn or downturn. Such a projection would be almost certain to be wrong beyond the fairly immediate future. If there have been cyclical trends in the past, it is almost certain that these will be repeated in some form in the future.

Where there are cyclical trends, it is often much more difficult to isolate and understand the driving forces. Ask all the major customers whether they can explain to you what drives their own market. What drives their market will also be a major driving force of your own market.

The driving forces may be very simple or very complex. Among the simpler of these forces are:

● Higher or lower interest rates
● A stronger or weaker pound
● Tightening or relaxing of consumer credit
● Rise or fall in company profits
● Rise or fall in business confidence

All of these and many more may have a hand on the wheel that drives your market.

The domestic property market provides an example of simple forces having a very direct impact. An estate agent experiencing the boom of early 1988 may not have fully appreciated how a major piece of impending tax reform was fuelling the market, but as 1989 progressed he would not have failed to associate the downturn in business with increases in the mortgage rate.

The process becomes more complex when several different factors interact together, or when there is a lengthy chain of events between prime cause and end result. Consider the following:

● Creating a demand for one product may reduce the money available for spending on other products. With consumer products there is always a finite amount of money for spending, so it is necessary to understand how ordinary people make spending decisions. Much of the boom in microwave oven sales in recent years has been financed by money that might otherwise have been spent on audio equipment or cameras, for example.
● The further removed you are from the final end-use market the more unpredictable market trends become. If you are

supplying raw materials or component parts to be used in someone else's product, which then finds its way along a wholesale and retail distribution chain before it reaches the final consumer, you will find that even very slight changes in final consumption lead to very big increases or decreases in demand for your own product.

This is a function of decision-making at each step in the chain. The most important of these is the side-effect of traditional stock control systems. At each stage in the chain, stock control systems typically overreact to changes in demand and cause the change to be amplified at each successive link back in the chain. A change of as little as 1 or 2 per cent in consumer demand can often lead to a change of 20 per cent or more in demand for raw materials, at least until stock levels have readjusted themselves.

• Where the reaction to changes in demand is to adjust market price levels, the change in price will in turn cause further changes in demand. The result is a spiral effect, downwards or upwards. The influence of speculators in a market may compound such an effect.

Case study—complex driving forces Understanding how complex forces interact is not easy. One example will indicate just how complex this can be. In the aluminium distribution market (Fig. 9.1) the largest volume market sector was aluminium sheet. Figure 9.2 shows how a number of different factors interacted to drive this market sector in the early eighties.

This was a simple business. Distributors bought sheet from rolling mills across Europe, put it into stock and then resold it at a percentage mark-up to customers.

About three-quarters of the mill selling price represented the cost of aluminium ingot. The price the mills paid the ingot producers for ingot moved in line with the London Metal Exchange price.

The exchange price moved in a cyclical manner. When the world-wide demand for ingot moved ahead of supply the price

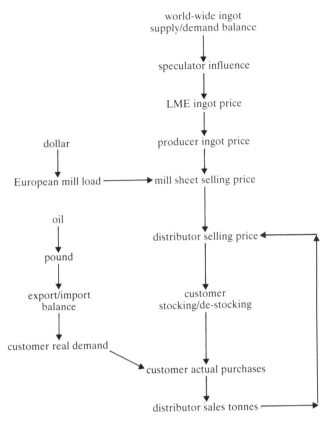

Figure 9.2   Forces driving aluminium sheet market

would rise. When the reverse happened the price would fall. These changes took place on a cycle of three to four years.

In a rising price market speculators entered the market and their purchases fuelled the price rise. In a falling market they unloaded their investments and helped the price spiral downwards. The result was that over a three-year period the mill selling price of aluminium sheet could change by over 50 per cent, following the ingot price cycle, even though none of the costs in the chain of production had altered.

When the dollar was strong European mills' exports to the United States soared and they quickly reached capacity limits.

They then aimed at maximizing their selling prices. When the dollar weakened the reverse took place and the mills would look for business at marginal prices to help fill up their capacity.

These two factors of ingot price and mill loadings governed the distributors' buying price and therefore also their selling price. Because all this was understood by major customers, these customers bought ahead of requirement to beat price increases in a rising market, and delayed reordering in the falling market in the expectation of buying more cheaply a few months into the future. This had a major impact on the apparent level of demand.

In those days Sterling was very much an oil currency, and the movements in exchange rate between Sterling and the European currencies affected the export competitiveness of the distributors' major customers. That accounted for the major part of the change in end-customer sales and hence in their real demand for aluminium sheet, although this was disguised by their re-stocking and de-stocking tactics.

When the distributors' sales fell significantly they would reduce the selling price in order to de-stock and keep working capital under control; and when sales were healthy they would raise prices to maximize gross margins. This pricing action in its turn had a compounding effect on the customers' de-stocking/re-stocking decisions.

The net result of these driving forces was a cyclical pattern, in which the level of annual sales bore no simple relationship to any of the indices of manufacturing output in the United Kingdom.

In that example the real driving forces were:

- World-wide balance between ingot supply and demand
- Dollar/Sterling exchange rate
- Price of North Sea oil

In any long-term planning it would have been necessary to rely on expert forecasts of the future trends of these three items. For more short-range forecasting it was possible to relate more directly to:

- LME ingot price
- European mill capacity utilization
- Sterling/Deutschmark exchange rate

What Is the Natural Geographical Market?

Almost every business has a natural geographical market. You may not be able to draw exact boundaries, but it is determined by:

- The number of potential customers and how they are scattered. The more customers there are, or the lower the price of your product, the more local in extent will your market be.
- The number of suppliers and where they are located in relationship to the geographical distribution of customers. The fewer suppliers there are, or the more specialized your product is, the wider will the market be.

For example, an estate agent may have a local geographical market, perhaps only one suburb of a large town, but the manufacturers of jet aircraft have a world-wide market. Only prejudice will make you travel 10 miles to a Sainsbury superstore if there is a Tesco just along the road, but if you are buying long-haul jets, there are only three suppliers in the world.

You cannot spend much time in a business without developing a feel for where these boundaries lie. Even if you only plot on a map the locations of the competitors you encounter most frequently, you will see some boundary take shape. Once you stray outside of this natural market boundary, a number of things happen:

- The costs of selling increase.
- The costs of after-sales service increase.

There comes a point where these costs start to rise so rapidly that the law of diminishing returns is experienced.

Provided that there is no difference in the product most customers will prefer to deal with a local supplier. Once you are selling too far outside the natural boundary it becomes necessary to make many more sales visits to a customer or to offer a price inducement just to counter the barrier of a closer competitor. The distance factor normally also means that less selling is done in a day than if you are operating closer to base.

The only way to extend your natural boundaries effectively is to establish additional operations that can provide at least as good a level of service as exists in the local market. Many people assume that just because the European single market is imminent this automatically means that their market will become the whole of the EC and not just the United Kingdom. Unless the natural market is already European-wide you will not succeed simply by sending in a sales team. You may have to consider a new manu-facturing or service base as well.

HOW ATTRACTIVE IS THE MARKET?

The fact-finding and analysis thus far should be starting to help you form a view as to how attractive each of your market sectors is. The factors affecting market attractiveness are summarized in Fig. 9.3. The view you form will play an important part when planning the strategy for recovery. There are a number of items in Fig. 9.3 that have not yet been investigated, but these will emerge as we move on in the next chapter to study the industry structure.

Market size	small .... medium .... large
Growth rate	low .... average .... high
Profitability	low .... average .... high
Competition	intense .... average ..... fragmented
Cyclical trends	yes .... no
Substitute products	yes .... perhaps .... none
Gaps in market	no .... perhaps .... yes
Market is:	unattractive .... attractive

Figure 9.3   Market attractiveness

10

Understand the industry structure

The market-place we have studied in Chapter 9 is a bit like a board game. It is a certain size, it has so many squares and there are rules that condition the movement of pieces between the squares. In this chapter we shall look at the players on the board. There are three categories of players:

- Customers
- Competitors
- Suppliers

Just as you can take different routes across the board game, so there are different ways of getting products to the customers. We shall therefore also look at:

- Routes to the market

Then we shall examine two final aspects of this industry:

- What is new?
- What are the entry barriers?

THE CUSTOMERS

The importance of customers is self-evident and a soundly-based market strategy hinges on understanding them in some depth. We shall begin by identifying the potential customer base and then we shall quantify that. Finally, we shall ask some less quantifiable questions and it will be necessary to visit key customers to elicit the answers. The most important aspect will be to understand the customers' buying motives.

How Can They Be Identified?

There are many ways of identifying what the customer base comprises. The obvious starting point is:

- The list of existing customers
- Potential customers who appear on sales prospect records

That will almost certainly not be all of the customers in the market. At this stage you should do some more research, using the following sources:

- Trade associations, which may (or may not) be willing to supply their list of members.
- Trade or business directories, which you will find in a public library. The most complete customer list will always appear in the directories that do not charge companies for a basic entry listing.
- Trade magazines.
- Exhibitions.

These sources will help identify existing customers, but there may be potential new customers about to enter this market. Have there been any reports of new companies just about to set up, or of other firms about to diversify into this market? Apart from the fact that a major new customer could add significantly to the market size, there is also an advantage in getting your foot in the door before the building goes up.

Get your sales team to pay a brief visit to the estate department of all the new towns in their territory and to the property agents negotiating the leases on any new industrial estate. They may be a good source of advance information.

Having identified the existing and possible customers, this is what we need to know about them:

- How many, and what size are they?
- What is their annual spend?
- What is their market-place like?
- What are their buying motives?
- What is the cost of changing supplier?
- Are any likely to integrate upstream?

How many, how big or small?

The first things we should establish are these:

- How many customers are there? Are there only a few or are there many?
- Are they big or small, or do they range in size from a handful of big ones down to a longer tail or smaller ones?

If the market comprises only a few customers, like the motor car manufacturers, for example, then these customers will act like magnets to every salesforce in the industry. If these few customers are also very large, like the car manufacturers are, then they will have a very great deal of purchasing power, and will be in a position to dictate many things to you, including conditions of contract, quality systems and the basis for price reviews.

On the other hand, if the market comprises a large number of customers, particularly a large number of smaller customers, then they will not be nearly so visible. It will take much more sales research to track them down and it may be more costly to reach them, but once there you may find less competition.

What is their annual spend?

How big each of these customers is in terms of annual spend on your product is important. A good sales team should have this vital information readily available from their customer records. If they do not, sit them down at a telephone for a few days until they bring their records up to date.

Once the annual spend is known, a profile of the customer base can then be prepared in this way:

- List the customers in descending order of annual spend, stopping when you have accounted for 80 per cent of the total market. In most markets the 80/20 rule should apply, and you will find that 20 per cent of the customers account for 80 per cent of the total market size.
- Record against each your own company's annual sales.
- Calculate your market share customer by customer.

This will give a profile of the customers in quantitative terms.

The remaining factors are more qualitative or subjective, and it will be advisable to visit a sample of key customers and seek out this information face to face, rather than relying on the opinions of the salesforce.

What is their market like?

It helps understand customers if you understand their market. Most of the questions we asked about the market-place in Chapter 9 can also be asked about the customers' own market. The aspects that will have most significance for your own business are these:

- Is it a high-volume, price-sensitive market? If it is, this market sector may be much less attractive to you. An example of this is the consumer electronics industry, which in the United Kingdom is dominated by Japanese companies. As this market matures many products are reduced in price as competition for market share intensifies, and suppliers may be expected to help support these price reductions. When you are struggling to improve your own margins this is not good news, especially when there is also an insistence on high levels of quality and delivery performance.
- What is the typical unit selling price of the customers' end-product? And what is the typical selling price of your own

product, expressed as a percentage of the customer's selling price? The higher this percentage is, the greater will be the spotlight on your own selling prices.

The best chances of maximizing gross margins will exist when the customer is making a high-price product which is not price-sensitive, and when your own product is specialized and accounts for only a low percentage of the customer's product costs.

The buying motive

The most important qualitative factor of all is the buying motive. What is it that influences customers when they make buying decisions? The major buying motives, but not necessarily in this order of importance, are:

- Price. Many salespeople believe price to be a more important buying motive than it really is.
- Quality.
- Product technology.
- Delivery. In many cases, reliability of delivery promise may be more important than a short delivery lead-time itself.
- Before- and after-sales service. Before-sales service could include technical or design assistance, as well as the level of response to sales enquiries.

Some customers will operate a formal system when making buying decisions. If you want to supply IBM, for example, you first have to offer proof of the excellence of your product. Even then you may not get to the point of receiving sales enquiries unless they actually have a need for a new supplier—and that is not very often—because they are a very good customer and in turn help their suppliers to be good suppliers. If you do get past the start-line, then a formal evaluation system takes over in which their measure of the supplier's quality, price and delivery performance are weighed in the balance in order to decide how to award purchase orders.

What benefits are customers buying?

If you step back into the customer's shoes, what the customer is really buying is benefits. Every good sales trainer tells the class on the first day that they are selling benefits, and it is perfectly true. Understanding what benefits the customer is buying is perhaps the most important thing of all. If you understand this, and tailor your product or service specifications to add additional benefits, you will gain a powerful competitive advantage.

The buying motive is really being driven by considerations like these:

- Will this supplier give me the technical help that will allow me to get my new product ready in time for the big exhibition?
- Will this supplier provide the level of quality and delivery performance that will enable me to order 'just-in-time' without the danger of the production line stopping?
- Will this supplier's component enable us to extend the life in service of our product?
- Will this supplier's product enable us to design our own product more cost-effectively?

This is just a brief selection of the many benefits which in real life actually influence the decision to buy. In the market you are examining you will find that different customers perceive different benefits.

Can you segment them according to this yardstick? If you can, then you will be in a position to match these against the benefits offered by your product or service, and so identify market niches where you should encounter less competition and be able to attain above-average gross margins.

What does it cost to change suppliers?

The cost to a customer of changing suppliers will determine the following:

- How difficult it is for your company to capture a competitor's customer.

- How difficult it is for a competitor to capture one of your own customers.

There may not be any cost of changing suppliers. This will be particularly true if the product is an undifferentiated commodity, which can be sourced from a large number of alternative suppliers.

The cost of switching suppliers may be more significant if:

- There were development or tooling costs which were invoiced up-front. The cost of changing suppliers in this case may involve paying these charges a second time.
- The customer has to change the design of the product in order to take advantage of the benefits offered by the alternative service or product. Apart from costs of redesign, there are also costs associated with implementing an engineering change throughout the manufacturing system, plus the inevitable costs of obsolete stock of the old product at the point of change-over.
- There is a long-term contract to supply.

Are any customers likely to integrate upstream?

Finally, ask whether there is any danger of customers integrating upstream into your own business activity. If this happens, it can make quite a dent in the market. Apart from the potential loss of sales, the danger lurking in the wings is that they may become a competitor if they subsequently try to market any underused capacity they may have installed.

THE COMPETITORS

We shall begin by identifying who your competitors are. Next comes the task of acquiring information about them and their products. With this information we shall then seek the answers to a number of questions which will be of help to you in the next chapter when we assess how competitive your own market position is.

Identifying the Competition

The first step must be to identify just who the competitors are. There are many ways of doing this:

- Sales records should identify who won the orders you lost and perhaps even who was bidding for the business you quoted for.
- You should know who else your key customers do business with; if you do not know, then ask them.
- Your material suppliers may have the most comprehensive list, because your competitors are their customers.
- You will also find your competitors advertising in the trade press and you will run into them at exhibitions.

Sources of Information

Once the competitors have been identified, the next step is to find out a great deal more about them and the products they make or the services they offer. Yet again there are several alternative sources of information and you may have to resort to all of these in order to answer the questions we shall shortly be asking:

- The direct approach. It may surprise you how just how often you can get competitors' product literature simply by asking for it. Some may even part with their selling price lists or offer samples of their products.
- 'Bingo cards.' Return the 'bingo cards' in the trade magazines using your home address.
- 'Ghost enquiries.' Send out 'ghost enquiries', using a plausible cover story and either your home address or that of a volunteer. This may be the easiest way of obtaining a sales quotation.
- Customers and suppliers. A friendly customer can tell you a

great deal about those of your competitors he knows well. So can your suppliers. Customers and suppliers will certainly know more about the competitors than anyone in your own company. They will probably be the only sources able to give answers to most of the subjective questions which need to be asked.

- Competitors' staff. You may have the opportunity to interview, or even hire, people who worked for your rivals.
- The public records. The information that is available in the public records includes the annual report and accounts of recent years. Advice on how to acquire this can be found in Appendix 1.
- Annual report. In the case of a public company, the latest annual report can normally be obtained on request from the company secretary.

The public records   There is a number of things that will frustrate you when going through the public records:

- Many of the companies will not have filed their latest annual returns and so the most recent financial information available to you may already be somewhat out-of-date.
- The difficulty of disentangling group structures. You may find that the real picture you need lies buried in a parent company's records, or in a subsidiary's, and you may need to unravel the chain of ownership, piece by piece, and then do some more searches.
- Private companies may have opted not to disclose their sales turnover, and this is one of the key items of information you want from these records. There are several ways of estimating this, but the easiest is to list those that do disclose turnover and to calculate what their debtors are as a percentage of annual sales. You can then calculate an average for the industry and use this to work back to an approximation of annual turnover for those who have not disclosed it. There are possible pitfalls here if any of the companies are factoring their debts, or if their debtors include short-term loans to

other group companies, but your accountant should be able to help guide you through calculations like these.

What You Need to Know about Competitors

From these various sources of information you will now be able to deduce a great deal about your competition. We shall ask some key questions under five sub-headings, which will later help you compare your own company more easily with the competition:

- Structure of the competition
- Their product benefits
- Their cost structures
- Their routes to the market
- Other strengths and weaknesses or threats

Structure of the competition   The key questions are:

- Have you many competitors or just a few? Do any of them dominate the market? You should prepare a competitor profile. List them in descending order of sales turnover. You can then calculate their individual market share.
- Which competitors are growing and which are declining? A comparison of recent years' accounts will reveal this.
- Which sectors of the market are your competitors active in? You will almost certainly find that your real competition differs from one sector to the next. You may be surprised how few of them encompass exactly the same spread of sectors as you do.
- Have any of your competitors carved out niches in the market for themselves?
- What is the geographical extent of their activity?

Competitors' product benefits

- What have you learned about their product? Is it a 'me too' product or is it differentiated in some way from most of the alternative products? Does the competitor product or service offer the customer greater or fewer benefits than your own? Do they have the resources internally to develop or enhance the product technology?

● What do you know about their price structure? How does it differ from yours?

Competitors' cost structures

● Can you deduce anything about their cost structure? The competitor with the lowest cost structure will always have a powerful advantage in the market-place. In many cases you may not be able to deduce this from their accounts, but at least you should be able to calculate turnover per employee. This will be a reflection of many factors, but it may give you a pointer to their cost structure. Alternatively, you may get pointers to this by asking customers or suppliers to identify what equipment and process technology your competitors use.

● Are any of the competitors about to add new capacity or make investments that will reduce their cost structure?

Competitors' routes to the market

● What selling resources do they employ to cover this market?
● How powerful is their marketing or promotional back-up?
● What is their overall image in the market-place and how have they achieved this?

Other strengths, weaknesses, threats

● Are they becoming more profitable or less profitable? Can you deduce the reason for such a change? If you can, there may be a model you can follow, or avoid, yourself.
● Are they on a sound financial base? If they are, then they will be in a better position to secure future business growth and to develop new product technology.
● What are their strengths? These may well be a threat to you.

What are their weaknesses? There may be an opportunity for you to take advantage of these.

- What do you know about their activity in the market-place and what can you deduce from it? Can you identify what their strategy may be? Why has this company succeeded or failed?
- Are there any mavericks among that list of competitors? Are there any whose objectives are other than making profit or increasing the net worth of their business? These could be big threats, especially if they are part of an integrated group simply wishing to secure a downstream market for profitable ventures further upstream, or worse still, to enlarge the captive market for unprofitable upstream activities.

THE SUPPLIERS

In most businesses the supplier structure will be much less important than that of the customers and the competitors, but a major exception will be if you are in the business of distributing someone else's products.

The key questions you should be asking are these:

- How many potential suppliers are there? You are much more vulnerable if you have only a few, especially if they are large and powerful.
- What ties are there between the suppliers and your competitors? These may restrict your own activity. On the other hand unhappy partners can easily be separated. How easily can the suppliers change distributors, and vice versa?
- How secure are your own lines of supply?
- How do the suppliers rank in terms of the benefit provided to you? How good are their products? How good is their service? How do they rate in terms of price, quality and delivery performance? What technical help can they give? What marketing help can they offer?
- How much do they need new business? Have they new or underutilized capacity? This could either be an opportunity for you to take advantage of their need; on the other hand it

could be a threat to price stability while they fill up that capacity.

- Are any of them likely to integrate downstream into your own business activity? That could be a big threat to you.

ROUTES TO THE MARKET

Effective routes to a market are a key ingredient of success. If you are in the distribution business, then you have to consider your own company as part of the route to the market. For a manufacturing company the route to the market leads from its own doorstep.

There are two distinct types of route to the market:

- Marketing routes
- Channels of distribution

Marketing Routes

The marketing routes should enable the company to achieve three goals in sequence:

- Making the customer aware of the existence of your product or service.
- Persuading him to allow you to bid for his business.
- Getting the order.

The appropriate marketing route in any specific situation will be a combination of all or some of the following. They are all complementary to each other in terms of the three goals set out above:

- Advertising
- Public relations
- Field salesforce
- Mail shots
- Telephone selling
- Sales agents
- Distributors

All of these are routes to the market. The choice of exactly which ones you use, and in which proportions, will depend on the structure of the industry you have just examined. Many people view advertising and promotion as something distinct from selling, but in real life these are usually complementary routes to the same market.

There are other factors which may influence the selection of routes:

- The size of the customer base. The smaller the customer base, the more cost-effective it may be to rely solely on face-to-face selling. The larger the customer base, the more necessary it becomes to use some or all of the alternative routes in order to screen out the real or immediate prospects in order to contain the very expensive activity of selling in the field.

- Separation of specification and purchasing functions. This happens when a product designer specifies the product to be used and a purchasing department later chooses the supplier. Some companies may use external product design consultants. The routes to the specifier may not necessarily be the same as the routes to the buyer.

- Subcontracting. Having selected its suppliers, the customer could then require component parts to be delivered to one of its subcontractors who will be producing sub-assemblies. This is quite common in the consumer electronics industry. The subcontractor may have the freedom to re-source, and its buying motives may be different from those of the original equipment manufacturer. The routes to the subcontractors may differ from the routes to the main customers.

- Consumer products. With most consumer products the route to the market separates into two very distinct stages:
  - The retail outlets have first to be persuaded to display and stock the product.
  - Then the public have to be persuaded to buy it.
    The routes to these two will be very different indeed.

You should try to put together a picture of how the competitors select their routes to the market.

- How do they create awareness out there in the market? Can you estimate how much they spend doing it?
- What sort of profile do they create in the media? A low profile may indicate that they are satisfied with the share of the market they already possess. Some of the newer entrants to the market, or any who have major additions to capacity planned or newly installed, may be highly visible.
- Are there any potential ways of creating awareness that the competition have overlooked?
- How do the competitors go about the job of selling? How big are their selling resources? What control do they have over these resources? To what extent do they rely on agents or distributors? Does this vary from one geographical market to another? Is there a demarcation depending on the size of customer, size of order or type of product? How much loyalty do any agents or distributors owe to their principal? Are these relationships exclusive ones? Can you prise any loose? Are there alternatives not spoken for?

Channels of Distribution

The channels of distribution are the ways in which the product physically moves from the factory of origin to the final customer. You must establish:

- What the pattern within the industry is. Is all distribution direct from factory to customer? Or are there regional or local distribution centres? Do these break bulk or do they preserve unit loads? Are they merely sorting depots or are they holding stocks to increase the local level of service? Are they fully owned and integrated or does the distribution channel pass through independent wholesale and retail chains?
- What transportation methods are used at each step in the chain.
- Who finances any inventories in the distribution pipe-line.

- If there are multiple channels being used, what percentage of the market is served through each channel. How do the various channels differentiate between type of customer, type of product or order size? If the pattern is other than very simple you must map it out, competitor by competitor, if necessary.
- Whether these choices of channel change as they move from a home market to more distant or export markets.
- Why these channels have been set up the way they are. Are they market-driven to maximize customer service? Or are they cost-driven to reduce unit costs of distribution? Or a trade-off between the two? Sometimes compromise solutions can expose a weakness for others to exploit.
- How well these channels actually function. Are they cost-effective?
- Whether there are any significant gaps in the distribution map.

UNDERSTAND WHAT'S NEW

What is new within this industry will fall into two categories:

- Innovation
- Product substitution

Innovation

The ability to innovate is a major strength. Companies that are successful in innovation possess a major strategic advantage. Ask the following questions to understand what is new:

- What innovations are taking place in this market?
- Have any of the competition developed a new product technology that adds substantial benefit to the product? Is this home-grown or is it available from independent sources?
- Are there new process technologies that will significantly lower the costs of production?

- Do any of the suppliers have new materials that can either add to the product benefits or lower the material costs?
- Is the customer's technology or product design about to change? What effect will this have on future demand for your product?

Product Substitution

In the previous chapter we have seen how product substitution can be a major driving force during the growth stages of a new market. You must now ask:

- Are there new products which may become substitutes for your own product? Or are there still more products which yours can replace? A good place to ask this question will be in the design departments of your major customers.
- Even more important could be to understand whether your customers' own products are themselves threatened by product substitution.

ENTRY BARRIERS

What are the barriers to a new company entering the market? The importance of this can be two-fold:

- If the barriers are high, it may inhibit you from entering new markets. Conversely, that may prevent new competitors emerging as additional threats to you.
- Low entry barriers may encourage many additional competitors to enter the market easily or frequently.

There are different types of entry barrier:

- Investment barrier. How much capital investment is needed? What fixed costs would be incurred before one unit of sales was produced? What level of sales would then be needed to break even? How much market share does this represent?

The higher this figure is the greater the barrier will be to a new entrant, and the less likely it will be that new competitors will emerge. But if one does, then it is going to be fairly big and it will have a very compelling need to establish itself quickly. This may not be good news for the existing players.

On the other hand, if break-even can be attained from a relatively low market share, then you can expect new competitors, small as well as large, to pop up with a fair degree of regularity over the future. Just how much of a nuisance this will be will depend on how fast the market is growing and how quickly they sort themselves out into niche market sectors.

- Technology barrier. This may be product technology, process technology or materials technology. How difficult is it for potential competitors to acquire this technology? How easily can it be copied? Are there any patents, copyrights or licensing agreements in force?
- Distribution barrier. Are the existing channels closed to a new entrant? Or are there independents who are free to serve a newcomer? If none is available, how costly will it be to create a new distribution network?

Most of the questions asked in this chapter will do no more than give you a picture of the structure of the industry as it is today, or perhaps even only as it was some time ago when the information you have acquired was compiled. The industry structure, just like the market itself, is never static: it is constantly evolving. You will never be able to predict with complete certainty what future shape the structure will take. The best you can do is to stop and think very hard about the questions that relate to the future. To be forewarned is to be forearmed.

All of this information is taking us closer to answering those key questions posed at the end of Chapter 8. You will already have gleaned some new information which will have helped you come closer to completing the analysis of market attractiveness you began in Chapter 9. In the next chapter we shall move closer to home and put the spotlight instead on your own business. That will take you on the way to answering the rest of those key questions.

11

Understand your own company

Now we are going to get closer to the real nub of the problem. In the last two chapters you have gained an insight into both the market-place and the industry structure within that market. In this chapter you will put your own company under the microscope. What has been learned about the competition will enable you to compare your own company to your competitors and so assess how competitive your own position is.

We shall begin by summarizing what is already known. Then we must seek some more basic data. After that we shall address four of the crucial questions stated in Chapter 8:

- How competitive are your product benefits?
- How competitive is your cost structure?
- How effective are your routes to the market?
- How effective is your organization?

As we answer these questions, we shall consider the ways in which your competitive position could be improved. We shall also ask how innovative your company is.

WHAT YOU ALREADY KNOW

From the work already done in previous chapters you already know a very great deal about the company:

- With the help of the management accounts, cash flow statements and the balance sheet, you know just how serious the position is and how much time you have in order to complete the recovery. Since putting the survival plan into action, the performance of the company will have improved, but you may still have limited time at your disposal before the funding dries up.

- You have learned something about the past history of the company (Chapter 3). You may find that explains much of what you are now about to unearth in this chapter. Understanding how things have happened, and why, always helps put them properly in context.

- You know what the break-even point is. The action taken in the survival plan may have moved the break-even 'goal-posts' closer within reach.

- You formed an approximate idea of production capacity (Chapter 4). By now you may have spent time calculating this more precisely. In the process you should have found out which, if any, of your production processes or work centres is the bottleneck to increasing capacity. You should certainly have calculated the cost of marginal increases or decreases to production capacity, and just how far you can go before you hit the bottleneck, and so incur a major incremental step in costs. You should also calculate what that major step in cost does to the break-even point.

- With the help of a spreadsheet you may even have worked out what production capacity is, given varying combinations of sales or product mix.

- Regular monitoring of the key performance indicators (Chapter 7) should have helped add to the understanding. You should at least have the measure of delivery performance, quality performance and production efficiency by department or work centre.

- The product costing system (Chapter 7) will now be starting to provide reliable data and we shall be making a lot of use of that over the next few chapters.

OTHER BASIC DATA ABOUT THE COMPANY

There are some basic data about the company which you should assemble and record at this point:

- What is your market share?
- What is your growth rate?
- What market sectors do you serve?
- Who are your major customers?
- Who are your major suppliers?
- What is your product profitability?

What Is Your Market Share?

How big or how small your market share is, and how it compares to the major competitors, will have a major bearing on any strategy you formulate. You should calculate market share both by volume and by value. We have already seen (Chapter 9) that in some instances measuring this by volume may be neither appropriate nor possible, but where it is available then both will be relevant.

What does the comparison of the two figures indicate? If you are doing better in volume terms than in value terms, but have only a low market share, you may have a very big problem indeed. It would indicate that the company is a small force in the undifferentiated end of the market, and that is not a very tenable position to be in.

What Is Your Growth Rate?

This too you should know by volume and by value. It too will have a bearing on the future strategic direction you take.

How does your growth rate compare to the growth in the total market? In a growing market you would normally expect companies with a low market share to increase their share at the expense of the market leaders, while in a declining market the leaders would normally maintain their volume, thus squeezing some of the smaller fry out of the market altogether.

What Market Sectors Do You Serve?

You have already identified these when defining the business you are in (Chapter 9). Most of the recovery strategy will be considered at this level of detail, so it will help if some more information is to hand at that stage.

You should now calculate market share and growth rate, sector by sector. Do you know, or can you estimate, the profitability of each sector? You may be serving too many sectors or too few sectors. Too much of the effort and too much of the costs may be concentrated in the less profitable sectors.

Who Are Your Major Customers?

Make a list of the major customers showing annual sales volume and value. What share do you have of each of these customers' total business? What percentage of your own production capacity does this represent? There is a high risk in being over-dependent on a small number of large customers, especially if you already have a high share of that business. It is much more comfortable to have risks spread more widely.

Who Are Your Major Suppliers?

List the major suppliers by annual volume and value, just as you did with the customers. What share does each have of your business? What percentage of their capacity does your business represent? There is a big risk in becoming over-dependent on a small supplier or in allowing a large and powerful one to gain too much of a leverage on you.

What Is Your Product Profitability?

We have already seen how the mix of products with different gross margins affects break-even (Chapter 4). A key factor in reshaping an ailing business will be to enrich the product mix. This may involve discarding low-margin products, which are a drain on the business resources. We shall therefore rely heavily on product profitability information when preparing the strategy for recovery. To be of maximum use this should be assembled in the following way:

- List all the company products and against each one record the following data:
  - Annual sales value.
  - Total gross margin. The products with the highest total gross margins will be recovering the greater part of the company's overhead costs.
  - Gross margin percentage. The products with the highest gross margin percentage will be the ones that enrich the product mix and recover overhead costs the fastest.
  - Gross margin per unit of effort. This will indicate which products produce the greatest margin for the least production effort. This should be calculated with reference to the specific situation in the company. If the production process is labour-intensive, it should be the gross margin per direct hour or per pound of direct labour cost. If one of the key production processes is the bottleneck to overall capacity, base the calculation on a direct hour or pound cost in this department alone, if the costing system permits. If the production process is more automated, calculate instead the gross margin per machine-hour in the core production process or in the bottleneck process.
- Rank the products in descending order by each of the three measures of gross margin. It is most probable that the order of ranking in the three lists will differ quite significantly from each other.

  Using a comparison with historic sales data, you should also be able to ascertain whether, after allowing for inflation, the product mix is becoming richer or weaker.

Thus far the new information gathered is reasonably quantifiable, so long as the product costing system is reliable. Now we enter a more subjective realm where it is necessary to make comparisons based on information which itself may be subjective.

The key to having a competitive advantage will depend above all on two factors. These are:

- Customers buy benefits. This means that the more benefits your product or service offers, the stronger your competitive position will be.
- The competitor with the lowest cost structure holds a position of great advantage in the market.

What we must now do is to see how your products and your company stack up against these two key criteria. As we go along we shall ask what can be done to improve the position on both counts. This will lead into a management audit of a number of key aspects of the business.

ANALYSE YOUR PRODUCT BENEFITS

We have examined the customers' buying motives (Chapter 10) and discovered that it is really benefits that they are buying. Then we studied your competitors' products, identifying what benefits these provided. What you must now do, for each market sector, is this:

- List the buying motives in descending order of importance.
- Write beside each buying motive what benefits can be provided by the product or service that satisfies that buying motive.

For each benefit now ask two questions:

- How well does your product or service provide that benefit?
- How do the benefits you offer compare with what is offered by your competitors?

An easy way to do this is to make a column for each competitor and use a simple marking system, like points out of ten, or one to

Table 11.1   Competitive position: product benefits

Buying motive	Product benefit	Ourselves	Competitors				
			A	B	C	D	E
a	p	**	****	*	***	*****	***
b	q	*	***	****	***	***	**
c	r	**	**	*****	****	****	***
d	s	***	***	****	***	****	***
Summary		**	***	****	***	****	***

five stars, covering the spread of answers from extremely well to not at all. This analysis could resemble the one in Table 11.1.

When this is completed, you will have little difficulty in forming a sufficiently realistic view of the competitive strength or weakness of your own product and service compared to those of the competition.

How Can You Offer More Benefits?

Once that analysis is done we must then ask: What can be done to raise your own rating to nearer the top end of the competitive spread? This will lead into a fairly thorough audit of many of the functions within the company. Here are some of the areas which you may need to examine in some depth.

Product mix   Do you have sufficient breadth? And sufficient depth? Other things being equal, it is less work for buyers to deal with those suppliers who can offer a full product range and a wide selection of features or options. Your product mix must be structured to take heed of what the market wants to buy.

Product technology   How well equipped are you in terms of R & D and product design? Does your product design need rethinking? Can you buy in the product technology you need? You do not need vast resources to add technology to a product. There may be small specialist companies that can supply a technology at least as good as the market leaders achieve with their in-house R & D departments.

Customer service   How easy or how difficult is it for the customers to do business with you? Are you providing adequate technical sales support? If you offered more, would this increase the benefit to the customer? Do you respond quickly enough to sales enquiries? If not, you may need to streamline the cost estimating and sales quotation systems.

Pricing policy   Are you pricing correctly? It is just as bad to underprice as it is to overprice. A badly structured price-list can mean that you lose out on large orders *and* make too little margin on small orders. Do you need to structure selling prices to take greater account of the segmentation in the market-place?

Delivery performance   How good is your delivery performance? Do you know what the market expects in the way of delivery times? Are you offering that? There may only be a very marginal sales advantage in offering shorter delivery times than the market needs. What may be much more important is to adhere to the delivery promises and to avoid under-deliveries. If delivery performance is a problem area, then you may have a lot of work to do on the production planning and control systems.

Company systems   The problem may have its roots further back than the shopfloor. Does it take too long for orders to reach the production department? That will mean some upgrading of the order processing system. Is the production department being held back by delays in a pre-production area? Or by materials not being available at the right time? If that is the case, work is needed in the area of MRP (material requirements planning), stock control or purchasing.

Quality performance   Are you falling down on quality? If so, does the problem lie in areas like life in service, failure rate in service or batches being rejected by customers' goods inwards inspection? Depending on the answer you may have to rethink the product design, tighten up inspection procedures or even revise the entire quality system. Perhaps it is a 'software' problem. Is after-sales service lacking in some respect?

Quality assurance Are customers now demanding that you have BS.5750 registration? When many companies achieve this themselves, it may be a requirement of their quality system that they then do business only with suppliers who also have BS.5750 registration. If you do not, then you may have a very major project indeed lying ahead.

Channels of distribution Do your channels of distribution work efficiently? Is the level of inventory in the distribution channel sufficient, and in the right places, to give the level of service the market needs? Is the service fast enough and reliable enough? If there are shortcomings in this area, you may need to bludgeon more than one distributor into making improvements. Can you supply them with a common system to help them all perform better?

In your business you may end up examining all or some of these key areas. You may very possibly find many more that are quite specific to your business. It is a bit like going through the check-list at a medical examination.

ANALYSE YOUR COST STRUCTURE

Now understand your cost structure, but more specifically compare this to your competitors' cost structures. This may be a very subjective comparison unless you belong to a trade association that collects and distributes to its members comparative data of this type. Failing that you must fall back on what you have gleaned from the competitors' annual accounts or what you can learn by asking customers and suppliers what they know about the competition.

You must understand what drives your own costs and why particular costs have moved up or down. Most important of all will be to ask:

- What is different between your cost structure and those of your competition?
- Why does it differ?

You should make this comparison over the major cost headings that appear in the management accounts. The most meaningful comparison may be to examine costs per sales unit or per pound of sales turnover, rather than taking percentage of sales turnover. Put this comparison down on paper in much the same way as you did in Table 11.1 (page 157), when the product benefits were being compared.

How Can the Cost Structure Be Reduced?

In looking for ways to reduce the cost structure there are some very obvious areas to explore:

Fixed costs   Do you have high fixed costs? You may be in a high-rent area or you may be in the wrong premises. Relocation or sub-letting may have to be considered as possible options.

Overhead staff levels   Are there too many people? You may be able to subcontract some functions and reduce both the head-count and the costs. Very small companies can function with a bare minimum of management and overhead staff. Much larger companies can afford highly structured organizations. In the middle ground the danger quite often is that you are just too big to run the business from 'the back of an envelope', but too small to enjoy the economies of scale that may be needed to justify the necessary management structure.

Overhead structure   Overhead costs may be too high because you are trying to be all things to all people. How much simpler would your overhead structure be if you concentrated on a narrower product mix, or if you concentrated only on the core process or final assembly, where the real value is added, and contracted out much of the upstream component manufacturing? Contracting out has the additional advantage that it places the onus on the out-contractor to respond to changes in demand levels.

Material costs   Are your material costs high in relation to your competitors? There may be nothing wrong with this if you are making a higher technology product requiring high performance materials. But there may be other reasons. Can you redesign your product and so design out some cost? Also, look back to your analysis of major suppliers. Are you using your purchasing power in the most effective way?

Direct labour costs   Do your rates of pay differ from those of the competition? Does this reflect differences in the levels of skills? Can you reduce costs by achieving greater flexibility, by having more people with multiple skills who can be moved to where work is needed, rather than having rigid departmental or skill boundaries?

Distribution costs   Lastly, put the distribution costs under the microscope in much the same way.

This type of audit of your comparative cost structure will lead very swiftly to a number of key areas, which we shall now consider more specifically.

Process technology   What is the state of your process technology? Is it capital-intensive or is it labour-intensive? Are your production costs too high because your competitors have installed more automated equipment than you possess? Are you suffering from under-investment in the past? What will it cost to trade up your technology?

Production engineering How good is your production engineering? Do you always find the least-cost production routes? What proportion of the shopfloor staff is actually making things, as opposed to moving or handling things? Many companies fall down, even with state of the art machinery, just because they concentrate only on the process and ignore materials handling and the efficient flow of materials throughout the factory.

Productivity Do you have a productivity problem? If so, do you know what is causing it? Is it poor production engineering, which means that too much work is needed in the first place? Or is production efficiency below standard? Have you a measurement of production efficiency, department by department? The bottle-neck department is the most critical. Or do you simply have too many people running the production equipment?

Production efficiency Understand what is driving the production efficiency level. Is the basic work-rate machine-driven or is it labour-dependent? If it is labour-dependent, a lot will depend on the quality of your supervisors and on how well the operators have been trained in their job. How dependent is efficiency on the organization and flow of work? How is it influenced by quality? Every minute spent on rectification or rework reduces your overall productivity.

Idle time Too often people assume that raising efficiency means making the operators work harder. If you had visited a German factory in the late seventies, when Britain was the 'sick man' of Europe, the first thing that would have struck you was that workers on the factory floor worked no harder than their British counterparts. The major difference was that they worked produc-tively for a higher percentage of the time. Take a hard look at your systems. Can you reduce the idle time caused when materials do not turn up in the right place at the right time, or when the next job is not to hand when the operator finishes the previous one?

Quality costs   Do you understand your quality costs? High reject rates are very often a major reason why costs are too high. Poor quality leads to excessive material costs and to excessive direct labour costs. If the only way you can deliver an acceptable quality level is to screen out the rubbish, then you have yet another excess cost in the inspection department. Do you have a quality system? Is there a culture of 'getting it right first time'? Do *you* believe in the need for high quality? The quality culture begins with the boss's attitude.

What drives quality?   You must understand what really drives quality in the company. Are the production processes automated? If so, are they reliable enough to deliver a level of quality that is being driven by the basic capability of the machine? In that case you may be able to operate an SPC (statistical process control) system, with final inspection limited to sampling to an appropriate AQL (acceptable quality level). Or are you labour-intensive, with quality being subject to the random effect of operator performance? In this case investment in more automated equipment will have a two-fold justification. In addition to increasing productivity, it should also bring significant reductions in quality costs.

Interest charges   How badly is your comparative cost structure being eroded by interest charges? We looked at this in Chapter 3 (see page 36). There may not be much you can do to lessen the effect of the cumulative losses you are funding, which is a millstone your competitors probably do not have, but you must focus on the extent to which your interest charges are being influenced by working capital.

Just calculate your working capital as a percentage of annual turnover. Do the same for your competitors. How do you compare? We saw in Chapter 5 what can be done to lessen working capital requirements, but let us put the importance of this in some perspective.

Here is a comparison of the stock levels of four companies, which make process control equipment. The figures are from their 1986 accounts:

	Stocks £000	Annual sales £000	Ratio %
Company A	28 966	52 700	55.0
Company B	1 276	11 100	11.5
Company C	2 333	5 600	41.7
Company D	323	2 500	12.9

If companies A and C had been able to operate on the same relative stock levels as companies B and D, then with interest rates at 16.5 per cent their savings on interest charges would have enabled them to reduce their selling prices by up to 7 per cent without affecting their profit. In the case of Company A (a British company) this action could very well have squeezed a number of competitors out of the market.

This is what a JIT (Just-in-Time) system can achieve. It can fund price reductions by reducing the money tied up in inventories. It enabled Japanese companies to grow at the expense of weaker competitors without sacrificing profitability in the process.

HOW EFFECTIVELY DO YOU REACH THE MARKET?

With a problem company you must have been prepared to find a great many areas which had shortcomings that put you at a competitive disadvantage. If you were to put all the wrongs right, and so gain a position of relative advantage, it would still be of little use unless you could also exploit such an advantage by reaching the market effectively.

The effectiveness of your routes to the market is therefore the next aspect of the business we must put under the microscope. Yet again, it is essential not only to assess how effective your routes are, but also to ask how effective they are compared to the routes of your competitors.

It is the marketing routes that are the more important at this point, and some of the aspects we must question are these:

Image   What sort of image does the company project? Is it positive, one that makes potential customers immediately add your name to their list of potential suppliers? This image is conveyed not just by advertisements in the media or by publicity material, but also by how the sales staff approach prospective customers. And this image has to contend with the image that lingers after a customer has done business with the company.

Brand names   Are your brand names good? Too many people overlook the importance of a good brand name, believing it only relevant when selling consumer products.

The sales message   Are you getting the sales message across to enough people? Have you chosen the most cost-effective routes to do that? Is the message getting to the right people? And often enough? Are you saying the right things? Are you selling benefits?

Selling resources   Have you sufficient resources to be doing all of that effectively? Could you achieve more with fewer resources if only they were directed and controlled more professionally?

Sales activity   Take time to assess whether or not your selling activity is adequate. Is it being directed towards achieving results? Or are too many of the salesforce just doing a 'milk-round'? Are all sales leads and enquiries being followed up? Is someone always asking for the order?

Sales management   Get out in the field with the salesforce. Are they managing their territories cost-effectively and maximizing their selling time? Or are there too many visits to customers too far away, at the seaside perhaps? Is each sales call planned before your salesperson steps inside the customer's door? Is the objective in making that call thought out? A call to get information can be just as valuable as a call to ask for an order.

Selling benefits   Is your salesforce spending more time talking than listening? Good salespeople do not need the gift of the gab. Quite the reverse. They ask important questions and spend most of their time listening. They know when to close. And how to close. Does your salesforce understand the product they are selling and its benefits? Are they aware of the customer's buying motive? Do they understand the customer's time-scale? Is it all in their records, with an action plan of what they must do next? In short, can they sell?

The answers to these questions may lead you to rethink your marketing approach, to upgrade your sales management, to retrain your salesforce or, in the worst cases, to get rid of some of your sales team. When preparing the survival plan we looked closely at barriers to sales. A bad salesperson is the most effective barrier of all, a barrier that prevents the customer from appreciating the company's product benefits.

DOES THE ORGANIZATION WORK?

Now put the company organization under the microscope. There are a number of prerequisites to an effective organization:

- Teamwork. Good organization is founded on teamwork. Are your people fighting the competition or battling among themselves? Who are the weak links? Are they in the wrong job? Or is it time they departed? Your own management style will be a major feature influencing good teamwork.

- Management control. Are your managers and supervisors really in control? If not, what is to be done to regain control?
- Reaction and decision-making. How good are the reflexes of the organization? Does the team react swiftly to problems? How fast are decisions made in the company? Or is there too much red-tape that could easily be done away with?
- Systems. For the most part the systems support the organization, and in many cases the computer is doing what people did not too long ago. The most important systems are those that make things happen, like getting the sales order into production, correctly and promptly. Where do you need to speed things up or give more accurate information to help avoid mistakes being made? The cost of implementing better systems can today be reduced by using a database language on a personal computer.

HOW INNOVATIVE ARE YOU?

Innovation is a very powerful strategic weapon. How innovative is your own company? Most people are followers rather than innovators, especially in problem companies. But ask the question nevertheless. Have you been innovative in new products, for example? Or in identifying and exploiting new markets? In finding new routes to the market? In introducing new technologies? Then ask the same questions about your competitors and see how you rank compared to them.

12

The strategy for recovery

INTRODUCTION AND OBJECTIVES

The objective of the strategy for recovery will depend on what the company position now is. If the survival plan led to at least a break-even position, the objective should now be to achieve whatever level of profitability will satisfy the shareholders. Where the problems were very deep-rooted, the survival plan may have served only to limit the damage, in which case the present objective may be to reach break-even point.

At this point it is worth restating what the essential ingredients are of a successful business:

- Competitive product benefits
- Competitive cost structure
- An attractive market
- Effective routes to the market
- An effective internal organization

The first four of these apply at the level of market sector, and it is at this level that much of the thinking will now be carried out. All of these aspects have been examined in depth in the previous three chapters. The exercise we are about to undertake will depend on a realistic assessment of each of them.

Figure 12.1 indicates the overall framework or methodology we shall use to prepare the strategy for recovery. We shall first evolve a market strategy for each market sector. We may decide to withdraw from some of these sectors. Finally, the individual

Step 1	market position = comparative benefits + comparative cost structure ↓
Step 2	strategic position = market position + market attractiveness ↓
Decision 1	lose/lose position? — yes → restructure no ↓
Step 3	key strategic questions = critical market sectors ↓
Step 4	success/fail path = strategic position + organization + routes to market ↓
Step 5	SWOT analysis = strengths and weaknesses + opportunities and threats ↓
Step 6	strategic problems ↓
Step 7	strategic options ↓
Step 8	evaluate the options = cost–benefit analysis ↓
Step 9	market strategy ↓
Step 10	recovery strategy = Σ market strategies + support strategy ↓
Decision 2	break-even?—no → restructure ↓ yes
Step 11	action plans ↓
Step 12	implement

Figure 12.1   Logical steps in planning recovery strategy

market strategies will be drawn together into an overall strategy for recovery. This must then be expanded into detailed action plans, which must then of course be implemented successfully.

Along the way we may reach a decision instead to carry out a complete restructuring of the business. This will be covered more specifically in Chapter 14.

The thought processes required during the exercise that follows are both demanding and specialized. This is where you may benefit greatly from external assistance. In any event the following are needed:

- An understanding of strategic principles. These are summarized in Chapter 13.
- A need for many different minds to tackle the exercise together. The way to do this is to set up a 'think tank', and we shall consider this presently.

Before this exercise it will be helpful to recap briefly on the subject of strategic direction.

THE CHANCES OF SUCCESS

In Chapter 8 we saw the alternative strategic directions plotted on the strategic compass. The strategy for recovery will consist very largely in selecting the particular strategic directions for each market sector, which when combined will lead the company to recovery. At this stage these choices of strategic direction can be presented more definitively in Fig. 12.2.

These varying probabilities of success are due to a combination of effort and risk:

- Market development. This implies finding new markets, perhaps some geographical markets ignored up to now, or finding new customers for existing products, or new distribution channels to take the product to the market. Or it may involve seeking out new or novel end-use applications for the products.
- Product development. This will lead along the trail of im-

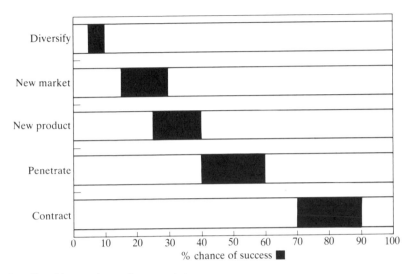

Diversify = New product and new market
Penetrate = Growth in same products/markets
Contract = Fewer products or markets

Figure 12.2   Probability of success of different strategies

proving products so as to enhance the benefits offered to
customers, or even providing new products to address their
needs in a different but better manner. Alternatively, it could
mean providing customers with new or better services or
offering a more comprehensive package of services.

• Diversification. You can see why it is that diversification has
  the lowest success rate. It carries all the effort and all the risks
  of both product development and market development at one
  and the same time.

• Market penetration. Deeper market penetration could mean
  relaunching products on the market or stepping up promotional activity, and perhaps become more aggressive. This
  may mean reducing unit costs so as to be able to cut selling
  prices.

All of these strategic directions involve courses of action that carry
substantial risks. That is why the chances of success are as low as
Fig. 12.2 shows.

- Selective withdrawal, on the other hand, leads for the most part through waters already known and which should be relatively clear of major risks. That is why it has a higher probability of succeeding.

In a loss-making company it is always best to avoid unnecessary risks. You simply cannot afford them. At the same time it would be foolish to ignore opportunities just because of the element of risk attached to it. Exploiting a big enough opportunity successfully could actually be the fastest route to success.

You will see now what von Clausewitz meant when he said that strategy is simple, but not easy. The options open to you are very simple and straightforward, but it is making the best possible choice of option which is far from easy.

There are three options, which did not appear on that strategic compass in Chapter 8, which may also have to be considered at some point.

- Closing the company.
- Selling the company.
- Merger or acquisition: this is really a logical extension of one or other of the three growth directions on the compass, and you may consider this as an option later.

Closure or sale are options which should loom up only if you cannot solve the problem by restructuring, or if the likely costs of recovery exceed the funds available. In the meantime the net worth of the company will be decreasing as each month's loss tots up. If nothing else, this puts pressure on you to complete the exercise in hand with the minimum delay.

SET UP A 'THINK TANK'

Planning the recovery strategy will be far and away the most difficult task in this book. It needs a great deal of creative thinking to be applied to it. This is where you may need to look for some more expert help. Above all, do not try to do it all on your own.

Get all of your management team to take part with you and if at all possible, get some unbiased outsider to sit in on this as well.

You would be well advised to assemble a 'think tank' behind closed doors, with no telephones ringing, for however long it takes to complete the exercise. All the members of this 'think tank' will need to have absorbed and understood the analyses of market, industry and company which have been completed over the preceding chapters.

THE PLANNING PROCESS

There is a number of logical steps to be followed in these think tank sessions. An overview of the complete process is shown on Fig. 12.1. The first two steps apply to all of the market sectors you identified in Chapter 11. From step 3 onwards you will become more selective and spend the greater part of the time working on only those critical sectors which are the key to your recovery. By the time you reach step 10 you will again be looking at the business as a whole rather than just at individual market sectors. Along the way you may discover that it is best to opt instead for a major restructuring exercise.

Step 1: Market Position

First identify your market position, sector by sector. Market position depends on:

- How competitive your product benefits are.
- How competitive your cost structure is.

These are questions that have been asked and answered in the previous three chapters.

The market position should be plotted on the simple diagram shown in Fig. 12.3. Do it on two steps:

- Product benefits. First fix a position on the vertical scale by assessing how competitive your product benefits are and

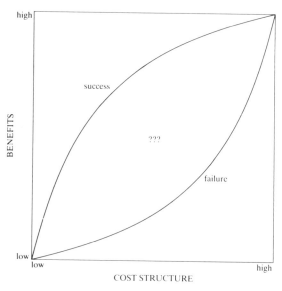

Figure 12.3   Market position

draw a horizontal line across the diagram from this point on
the scale. If your assessment had been similar to the one in
Table 11.1 (page 157), for instance, you might fix your
position about one quarter of the way up from the bottom of
the scale.
- Cost structure. Then fix your competitive position on the
  horizontal cost structure scale and draw a vertical line
  upwards from this point.

Where the two lines meet represents your market position. The
diagram is divided into three segments, labelled:

- 'Success'—the higher your competitive benefits and the
  lower your competitive cost structure, the more likely you are
  to attain success in this market sector.
- 'Failure'—the probability of failure increases as your
  competitive position weakens on both counts.
- '???'—in the middle ground is an area where you cannot be
  sure whether you will succeed or whether you will fail.

Your actual cost structure may vary from market sector to market sector, especially if you have different production lines or different production technologies for the various products. In many companies that will not be true. All the products may use common production facilities. If that is the case, then do not assume that the competitive cost structure is the same in each market sector. It will most probably vary considerably, depending on just who the competitors are in each of these sectors.

Using this diagram as an aid to strategic thinking depends on being realistic when you assess these competitive positions. What you have from the fact-finding is at best a subjective comparison. The worst thing you can do is to pretend that your competitive position is better than it really is.

There are a couple of useful ideas to bear in mind when plotting this diagram and others that follow in later steps:

- Invite all members of the think tank to do the exercise individually, and then chew the fat collectively until you reach a consensus view. That way at least everyone will have to stop and listen to why each person arrived at the answer each did, and the debate that follows may help pin-point the most realistic position of all.

- Have this exercise done on blank diagrams which omit the division into segments. That way you remove the temptation to pre-judge the answer. When all the team have plotted the market position as they see it, then you can transcribe all their answers onto one diagram with the three segments already drawn in. That may also help speed up the process.

Having done this for each market sector, you can then summarize the overall company position extremely effectively by plotting the market position of all the market sectors onto one diagram, and then drawing round each position a circle or square that is in proportion to its sales volume or sales value. Figure 12.4 shows how this can be represented.

What that diagram looks like will depend very much on

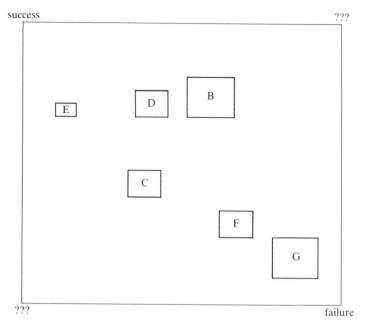

Figure 12.4   Overall company position by market sector

individual circumstances, but some general observations are applicable:

• If a majority of the higher-volume sectors in a loss-making business are in the segment labelled 'success', then think again. You may have been over-optimistic in assessing the market positions. The only other feasible explanation would be that you are in a strong competitive position, but are not reaching the market effectively.
• The further into the 'failure' corner a position is, the more certain it will be that both benefits *and* cost structure will have to be improved before the competitive position can move towards success. There is a high risk of non-achievement in having to tackle both fronts simultaneously. On the other hand, that risk may lessen if you start from a position in the middle ground. From there, a move in only one direction may take you into the segment of success.

Step 2: Strategic Position

The strategic position will depend on two factors:

- How competitive the market position is.
- How attractive the market is.

Market position has just been established in step 1, and we began to assess how attractive the market sectors were as early as Chapter 9. Your views will have become much clearer since then. All that remains is to summarize the position recorded in Fig. 9.3 (page 132).

The strategic position can now be plotted using Fig. 12.5.

- On the vertical scale plot the market position established from the diagram in Fig. 12.3.
- On the horizontal scale plot the assessment of market attractiveness.

The segments of this diagram will give a clearer idea of the chances of the possible ultimate success than we got by looking at market position alone. You will see now that there may not be a

Figure 12.5   Strategic position

lot of point in spending time and money to nudge the market
position into the success segment on Fig. 12.3 unless it means that
you also reach the success segment in Fig. 12.5.

A major difference between this diagram and the earlier one is
that on this one you can reposition only upwards or downwards.
You cannot change the market. This has fairly major implications
if you are positioned too far towards the bottom right-hand
corner.

Then, using the same method as in step 1, summarize the
position of all the market sectors onto one diagram (similar to Fig.
12.4). The end-product will be a diagram showing the overall
company strategic position and on which all the market sectors
are in position and represented by circles or squares in proportion
to sales volume or value.

Decision 1: Decision to Restructure

At this point you may well be in a position to start making
decisions. For example, if half or more of your sales volume lies in
the failure zone in Fig. 12.5, you probably have no choice but to
get out the surgeon's knife and start on a fairly major restructuring programme.

Even if there were other options open to you, that large a chunk
of business in a lose–lose area will be such a millstone around your
neck that it could very well prejudice the chances of overall
success. It will be much wiser to remove the cancer now.

If you do make the decision to restructure at this point, at least
your decision will be founded on unarguable logic and you will
not have foreclosed on a less painful and less costly alternative.

Not all loss-making companies will be in so extreme a position
as the one portrayed in Fig. 12.4. Suppose, for example, that only
a small percentage of the business is in that failure zone, and that
there is about as much in the success zone as in the dubious
middle ground. If that is true, then put the surgeon's knife away
for the time being. You may very well decide to vacate these
lose–lose market sectors, but you should probably be able to find
a recovery strategy that does not involve major restructuring.

Step 3: Key Strategic Questions

At this point a few key strategic questions arise out of that analysis of strategic position in step 2:

- Which markets should you concentrate on?
- Which products should you concentrate on?
- Which products should you withdraw?
- Where can you best use your scarce resources?

The diagrams you have just completed will be a pointer in the right direction. If there are some sectors that lie deeply buried in that failure zone, it may be wise to eliminate them from future plans here and now. The key to success will be in those market sectors that either lie in the 'success' zone or can be repositioned into the 'success' zone. Most of the action will need to be directed towards those that need repositioning.

Beware, however, of the danger of taking too narrow an approach. For example:

- How much of the total gross margin is at stake? Any sector that accounts for a significant portion of the total margin needs more careful consideration before you make the decision to eliminate it.
- Do not simply gloss over those sectors that lie fairly and squarely in the success zone. It is very tempting to assume that these will continue to succeed in the future. This could be incorrect. There may be a major threat on the horizon or there may be a big opportunity that could make such a sector even more profitable.

Step 4: Success/Fail Path

There is now a very simple model you can use to put each market sector into some kind of overall perspective. This is the 'Arrow Diagram of Success' (Fig. 12.6). In this model the flights of the arrow represent market position, the shaft is the organization and the arrow-head is the route to the market. The arrow's objective is

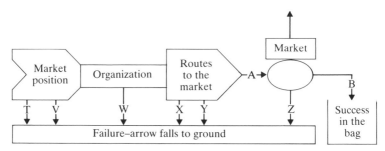

Figure 12.6   Arrow diagram of success

to get right to the heart of that market and land it in the bag labelled 'success'.

In this diagram, the route to success is the A–B–C flight-path. It represents a competitive market position, an organization that works well and an effective route to an attractive market. The arrow gets to the heart of the market and lands success in the bag.

The arrow can fall to the ground for a number of reasons:

- If your market position is weak because the product benefits are not competitive, the flights will come adrift from the shaft as the arrow is fired; that is route T.
- The same would happen if your cost structure is uncompetitive; that is route V.
- The shaft may break if your organization is weak; that is route W.
- You may not have an efficient route to the market or it may be misdirected; either way the arrow will miss its target; these are routes X and Y, respectively.
- If you hit the target, but it is a lead weight, then it may fall to the ground instead of into the bag, taking the arrow with it; an unattractive market is like this, and so you have route Z.

From what the think tank have learned so far, get them now to plot on this simple diagram which route is presently being taken in each market sector. It may be very subjective, but it is going to help point the next step more quickly in the right direction.

Does your arrow fall to the ground? Suppose you eliminated the reason for its falling to the ground, which route would it then take? Would it put the target in the bag? Or would it simply fall to the ground further along the flight-path? How many of the possible reasons for failure would you have to remedy before you got the arrow on the A–B–C flight-path?

You should not see route Z as irreversible. It may be possible to take aim at a more selective niche within that market.

Step 5: The SWOT Analysis

What you have just done in that simple exercise, albeit very subjectively and subconsciously, is to take account of a part of some very important factors; these are:

- The company's strengths and weaknesses.
- The opportunities open to it.
- The risks, or threats, it may be exposed to.

It helps at this stage if you write down what these are. This is known as a SWOT analysis (*S*trengths, *W*eaknesses, *O*pportunities, *T*hreats). You can do this on a large sheet of paper, ruled into four, as in Fig. 12.7.

To do this properly you may have to sift again through much of the analysis that has already been done.

The most common mistake in doing a SWOT analysis is getting confused between strengths and opportunities, or between weaknesses and threats:

- Strengths and weaknesses are things that relate specifically to your company.
- Opportunities and threats are things that exist out in the market or within its wider industry structure.

The following advice and comment may help your team during this SWOT analysis:

- Strengths. Be careful that you do not take too rosy a view of your strengths. What is important are *comparative* strengths,

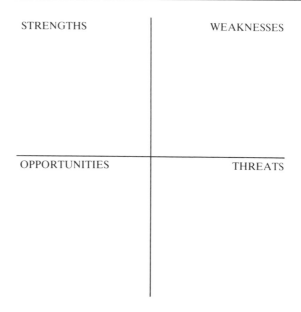

Figure 12.7   SWOT analysis

the areas where you are relatively stronger than the competition. For example, the fact that you have the very latest high-technology production process may only really be a strength if the competitors do not also have it. If they do not, then the possibility of their acquiring it may be a threat.

● Weaknesses. A weakness is a weakness, even if all the competition share that same weakness. The fact that they have the same weakness as you may be an opportunity, provided you correct your own weakness first.

● Opportunities. Many of the opportunities will fall out of your analysis of how attractive the market is, especially where there is growth or a gap in the market. Others may exist due to some weakness in the competitors' armour. The possibility of innovation on your part may be one of your biggest opportunities.

● Threats or risks. We have already noted many possible risks as we analysed the market and the industry structure. Your exposure to product substitution, to cyclical patterns, to possible new competitors and the risk attaching to your customer profile or your supplier profile could all very well be threats. So too could a major innovation by a competitor.

In doing this SWOT analysis you have to keep things in some perspective. The first time round you may very well fill several pages. Now go back and 'sore-thumb' it:

- Concentrate on what really is important.
- If an item is trivial, delete it.
- Unless you can establish cause and effect between what you have written down and the path the arrow took in Fig. 12.7, cross that item off the list.

The next step in the thinking will be far too complex if you have anything other than the really important items to take into account. Before you move on, ask how well this analysis stacks up against what you deduced in the arrow diagram in Fig. 12.7. If it does not stack up, then it is more likely to be this SWOT analysis that needs to be revised and not the arrow diagram.

The Importance of Synergy

Also go through the SWOT analyses of the different market sectors and make a list of all the strengths, weaknesses, opportunities or threats that repeat themselves.

In the textbooks you will find a lot of mention of 'synergy'. It can apply to expertise in the areas of process technology, product technology or to marketing and distribution. Synergy exists when a common technology enables you to attack more than one market sector using the same know-how. Putting it in simple language, it means killing many birds with one stone.

The items that repeat themselves in the various SWOT analyses may fall into that category. It may be a very important consideration later on, especially in view of the limited resources you have at your disposal.

Step 6: The Strategic Problem

From this SWOT analysis you should be able to define quite
clearly, after some thinking in depth, what the main strategic
problem is. There may well be more than one. Strategic problems
normally fall into these four categories:

- Strengths that have not been fully exploited
- Weaknesses that need to be corrected
- Opportunities that exist but have not been exploited
- Threats that exist or may soon exist

Identifying your own strategic problems may be easy or it may
need many hours of brainstorming. It is vitally important that
you get it right. This is where the outsider's point of view may help
you see things in a much clearer perspective than your own team
can. If you identify the wrong strategic problems, then you will, in
the next step, also identify the wrong courses of action; that could
prejudice the chances of recovery.

The summary of strategic principles in Chapter 13 may help
guide the thought processes at this point. It also contains models
for success that may be relevant to your own situation.

In pin-pointing the specific strategic problem, or problems,
that must be addressed, the most useful challenge will be to ask:

- How *important* is it?
- How *urgent* is it?

Those that are both important *and* urgent are the key problems.
Any that are neither important nor urgent should be discarded
from the list.

Step 7: Strategic Options

This next step in the thinking will also be difficult. You now have
to think through what the possible ways are in which you could
overcome the strategic problems identified in step 6. These are
going to be your strategic options. This is where it helps to have a
lot of creative or lateral thinking within the think tank.

Do not discard any ideas offered at this stage. Write them all down. Some may very well be fanciful or likely to break the bank, but these can be eliminated later on. Just make sure that all the options being offered are specific on two counts:

- *What* could be done.
- *How* it could be done. For example, 'increase sales' is *not* an option. It does not say *how* you would do it.

A brainstorming session should produce a wealth of options. Once the ideas stop pouring out, that may be a good time to call a halt and let everyone sleep on it overnight. Next morning someone should have thought of that major option you all missed and you will have a much clearer head when you start to work out what to do with this long list.

The main task will be to narrow down the strategic options quite considerably. To be a serious contender a strategic option must satisfy the following questions:

- Does it address the strategic problem?
- Is it feasible?
- Does it help create a competitive advantage for you? This may accrue from additional benefit to the customer, an improvement in the cost structure or greater effectiveness of the routes to the market.

The end-result will be a short-list of options. Before finishing, stop and ask whether you have looked hard enough for the really innovative option.

Step 8: Evaluating the Options

It will be necessary to make a selection from the short-list of strategic options identified in step 7. To help make that selection we will first subject each option on the short-list to an evaluation using a cost–benefit analysis.

To do this you must first estimate the costs and the benefits associated with each option:

- Costs: these will include both once-off costs and any new on-going costs. The once-off costs may be capital or revenue, or a mixture of both.
- Benefits: the benefits will be the change in gross margin generated or any reduction in on-going costs, or a mixture of both. To estimate the change in gross margin you clearly must forecast what the likely impact on sales and on selling prices is; you must also know the costs of materials and production.

These need only be estimates. It is not necessary to have precise figures, only to be in the right ball-park. But make sure you do not take too optimistic a view of things. If anything, err on the conservative side.

Good estimates will depend on a realistic assessment of the likely impact on the market position:

- Additions to product benefits. How significant will the improvements to the product benefits be which this option will allow? Just how much more market share will this allow you to capture? And at what selling price?
- Cost structure. You must consider whether you are going to take the benefit straight to the bottom line, or whether you are going to share it with the customers by way of price reductions in order to raise market share.

These evaluated options may now be subjected to a cost–benefit analysis in order to rank them in terms of effectiveness. We already have a model for this from Chapter 6, when the survival plan was being prepared. The steps you should now follow with each option are these:

- Make allowance for the probability of success, just as you did when making the survival plan.
- Project the cost–benefit analysis for at least two years ahead.
- Calculate the pay-back period. In a healthy business the rate of return on investment would be used to evaluate the strategic options. In a loss-making position this is academic.

You need options that quite simply yield sufficient benefit within the right time-scale. Instead of the rate of return, work out the pay-back period—the number of months it will take before cumulative benefit exceeds cumulative expenditure.

Step 9: The Market Strategy

The market strategy will comprise one or more of the strategic options already identified. From the evaluation made in step 8, we can begin that selection first by a process of elimination:

- In a loss-making situation you should discount any options that have a pay-back period of more than two years; in extreme cases nine months may be a more appropriate period.
- Discount any option that needs funding of the wrong order of magnitude. The once-off costs required to support the strategic options will need funding. Until you ask for new funding, do not pre-judge the answer, but you should have a feel for what is reasonable and what is not.

The short-list will be whittled down, probably to just a handful or so. These should then be ranked in terms of their relative cost–benefit. Your final choice is not limited to only one option, but if you select more than one, they must complement each other. They must not pull in different directions at the same time.

The option or options you have now selected is a market strategy for this market sector. It must pass some simple tests before you finally accept it:

- Does it 'feel' right? If it does not, then it is probably wrong and you should think again.
- Have you rejected any option with a greater cost–benefit than the ones you have chosen? If so, examine it once again before you discard it.
- Will this strategy be sufficiently flexible to allow you to react

to the many unexpected things that may occur along the way?
If not, then you should once more think again.

If it passes these tests, then at last you have a market strategy.

You must now repeat this process for each market sector,
arriving at a market strategy for each one. You must include any
sectors you are planning to eliminate. They will also have numbers attaching to them, both in terms of the gross margin you
sacrifice and the savings in overhead costs you will achieve as a
result of not competing in these sectors.

Step 10: Recovery Strategy

The overall recovery strategy will comprise the following:

- A market strategy for each market sector
- Any support strategies which may be needed.

Support strategies   Ask if there is anything else that may be needed
to support all or some of the market strategies that have been
prepared, especially action to eliminate general weaknesses in the
company. Or perhaps the market strategies have spin-off implications on other parts of the company, such as the organization
structure or in the production area.

If the answer is yes, then you must consider the options for
tackling these. You will go through much the same process as you
have just done in step 9, but it will be very much simpler and will
not take nearly as long. There are fewer intangibles to deal with.
This time you should select the most cost-effective of these
options. These will be the supporting strategies.

Decision 2: Does it Break Even?

Now use a spreadsheet once more and project forward what will
happen if you successfully implement this recovery strategy.
There are three important questions:

- Does it take you to a break-even position?
- Does it get you there within the right time-scale?
- Is the total funding needed within a sensible order of magnitude?

If the projection shows you only just falling short of break-even, or taking just a little longer than you would have wished, it is probably none the less a viable strategy, provided—and this is the crucial proviso—that you have consistently erred on the conservative side and not the optimistic side. A little further examination may highlight some possible cost-savings you had overlooked while focusing on the broader issues.

If you are a long way short of break-even within a realistic time-scale, by all means go back and reassess the hard work that has just been done. The great temptation, however, is that you will start massaging some of the numbers to arrive at the answer you want. If you find yourself doing that, call a halt and opt for a restructuring plan instead. Chapter 14 will guide you through such a plan.

Step 11: Action Plans

You now have a viable recovery strategy. The next step is to translate that into a set of detailed action plans. What is contained so far in the different market strategies is only the very bare bones or outline of what must be done. You must now think more deeply about each of your strategies and turn them into detailed action plans.

Each action plan must address the basics of What? How? Who? When? What cost? Do not forget to include milestones or benchmarks by which you can monitor progress and assess the overall success of each action plan. These action plans will need much more detailed financial forecasts than were made in step 8. In particular, they must become firm forecasts as opposed to estimates.

The formal plan you prepare will be similar in format and

content to the earlier survival plan (Chapter 6), and like that earlier plan it will serve the following purposes:

- Persuading the bank manager or shareholders to grant any additional funding needed.
- Communicating within the management team in order to reinforce the commitment to action.

Step 12: Implementation

Implementation is the most important step of all. This plan, just like the survival plan, will require sound project management. The difference is that this time there is likely to be much more in the way of action, requiring considerably more effort, and so there is a much greater need for professional project management.

If you need help or advice on that subject, you should find a good textbook or attend a short training programme. You may also find it helpful to use a PC-based project management system.

Many things will not go according to plan. Customers, suppliers, competitors and perhaps even the Chancellor of the Exchequer will all conspire to blow you off course. This is why the strategies needed to be flexible. When you hit snags you should persevere. Do not rush off to find a different strategy. Only do that if something so fundamental changes as to invalidate the strategy completely.

The best possible advice you could be offered is this:

- *The Will to Succeed is the Key to Success.*

13

The art of strategy

The chapter is intended to give you a basic appreciation of the subject of strategy, which may be helpful in the preparation of the strategy for recovery.

We shall start by looking at how the principles of military strategy developed and then follow through to the development of the principles of business strategy.

Finally, we shall look at well-tried models for success and, in particular, the best models for loss-making companies.

PRINCIPLES OF MILITARY STRATEGY

We have already noted in Chapter 8 that the concept of strategy had a military origin. Von Schlieffen, the architect of the military strategy that carried the German armies across Belgium in 1914, said that man is born a strategist, not made a strategist.

All the great battle commanders from earliest times were born strategists. Among the most successful were Julius Caesar, Genghis Khan and Napoleon Bonaparte. The brilliant success of Napoleon's early campaigns led many people to analyse what he had done in order to define a successful model for others to follow.

Two men in particular distilled Napoleon's success into principles of strategy which have guided military commanders right up to the present time. One was von Clausewitz, a name we have already encountered. The other was Jomini. It was his concept of the strategic compass that was borrowed to help begin the strategic thinking in Chapter 8.

These principles of strategy have been refined over the last century to take account of the technology of modern warfare and a very different world political scene, but the basic principles have changed scarcely at all since the days of von Clausewitz and Jomini. Today, the strategy taught at military academies across the world is virtually identical. A graduate of West Point will have learned the same basics of strategy as his counterpart at the Frunze Academy in the Soviet Union. The basic principles of military strategy are these:

- Focus single-mindedly on the ultimate objective.
- Concentrate your forces for attack.
- Attack the enemy at his weakest point.
- Choose the field on which you do battle.
- Take maximum advantage of the element of surprise.
- Maintain good communications with your combat forces.
- Make sure you have the resources to match your target.
- Use these resources as economically as possible.
- Do not over-reach your lines of supply.
- Make as much use of innovation as you possibly can.
- Plan every manoeuvre carefully in advance.
- Have the flexibility to react to the unexpected.
- Keep it all as simple as possible.

PRINCIPLES OF BUSINESS STRATEGY

Just as the famous military commanders were born strategists, so too were the founders of the great business empires. Andrew Carnegie, Henry Ford and Alfred Sloan were to business what Caesar, Genghis Khan and Napoleon were to warfare. It was Sloan's success at General Motors that in more recent times came to be used as a model for marketing strategy. In many ways he is to business strategy what Napoleon was to military strategy.

If you open any textbook on business strategy and look at the bibliography, you will find very little that relates specifically to business published before the early seventies. From then onwards there is a great flood of published work, and business strategy has become one of the keynote subjects in schools of business administration. Genghis Khan would probably be able to relate instinctively to much of what is taught today at the Harvard Business School.

Let us now take the principles of military strategy listed earlier and restate them as their equivalent principles of business strategy:

- Understand your objective. What business are you really in? This was the first question in Chapter 9. What is your *one* key objective? Higher profits? Increased profitability? Raising the net worth or share price of the business? Or growth? In your own case it may simply be to reach break-even.
- Concentrate your effort. Do not dissipate it by trying to go in different directions at the same time.
- Build on your strengths and avoid action that would expose your weaknesses.
- Take maximum advantage of a favourable competitive position and aim for the weaknesses of competitors.
- Seek out and exploit any opportunities that may be open to you. Identify and avoid threats to your business.
- Be a good communicator, so that everyone in the company clearly understands what must be done.
- Strike the right balance between your ends and your means. If you set your end-sights too high, your means may not stretch that far. Set your sights too low and there may not be a big enough challenge.
- Look for synergy. Find ways of using know-how or resources to support more than one activity at the same time. Kill as many birds with one stone as possible.
- Spread your risks. Do not become over-dependent on a small number of customers or suppliers. Do not put all your eggs in one basket. And avoid unnecessary risks.

- Be as innovative as you can. The most profitable changes always stem from innovation, but it has to satisfy one of three criteria we have already established:
  - Add to the customer benefits.
  - Make your cost structure more competitive.
  - Make your route to the market more effective.
- Build an effective organization. It must be motivated to the attainment of results. It needs to be good at decision-making. It has to be founded on good teamwork.
- Plan every step carefully in advance. Make it flexible. Keep it simple.
- Have the will to succeed. Keep at it until you do so.

These principles are in many ways motherhood statements. You probably take heed of a great many of them in everyday life without thinking about it. What is important now is that you take account of all of them together as you prepare the strategy for recovery.

MODELS FOR SUCCESS

As well as these principles there are a great many models for success, which have been seen to work, and you should look to these for guidance. The generally accepted models for success are these:

- Increase the customer benefits. As you increase the benefit to the customer, or as you improve product quality, this normally leads to an increase in profit, even at the prevailing market price level. This is because more competitive benefits lead to increased market share without a corresponding increase in the fixed cost structure.
- Reduce the cost structure. As the cost structure reduces and becomes more competitive, so profit increases. In a market that is price-sensitive, sharing part of the reduction in costs with customers will increase market share and will lead to an increase in profit that is greater than the reduction in costs.

- Increase the added value. The products with the highest added value yield the maximum profit for the least effort. Increasing added value raises productivity and leads to higher profit.
- Get the product mix right. Companies that offer a limited product range, but with comprehensive features aimed at a clearly-defined market sector, are more successful than those that try to be all things to all people.

These are the four most important models for success. There are some further models that apply depending on:

- Type of cost structure
- Market share
- The life-cycle status of the product

Cost Structure

High cost structure or high capital investment   As these increase so too does the break-even point. You will need a higher market share to make a profit. If you enter a new market, you will need to secure that high market share quickly. You will also need to offer a comprehensive product range and customer benefit package across a broadly defined group of market sectors in order to target a market big enough to justify the fixed costs or capital investment. High fixed costs or high capital investment normally result in lower profitability and lower return on capital employed.

Market Share

High market share   Companies with a high market share are usually more profitable than those with a low market share. Research has shown that there is a straight-line relationship between profitability and how big or small a company is in relation to its largest competitor. If your market share is much greater than that of the closest competitor, you will be much more profitable than you will be if you are only a small fry in a market dominated by much bigger competitors.

Aim for a high market share only if there is a high growth rate in the market or if the product is at the start of the product life-cycle. To succeed in this you will need very good market knowledge.

Vertical integration   There are many successful models of companies with a high market share improving profitability by integrating upstream, usually by acquisitions in the areas of component or materials manufacturing or in a pre-production technology, but these succeed best when retained as independent profit centres.

The same does not hold true about integrating downstream. In that direction failures exceed successes. This is usually because companies expect the downstream market to behave in the same way as their mainstream market. More often than not they are radically different.

Low market share   If you start with a low market share, any increase in market share will increase profits because the resulting increase in gross margin will be achieved without a corresponding increase in overhead or fixed costs. The quicker you use up any underused production capacity the faster the profits will increase.

From a low market share position you should avoid high R & D expenditure. Look instead for specialist suppliers to provide the technology the market leaders may have developed themselves. Concentrate yourself on making the product well and on tailoring the product features and product quality so as to maximize the customer benefits.

Companies with a low market share need above-average management. They must also keep a tight rein on marketing costs.

Niche markets   The most profitable route with a low market share is always to find a niche market and to work very closely with key customers to build a base of customer loyalty. The more you concentrate your effort into selective niches the more successful you will be. Diversification dissipates this effort and is a recipe for disaster.

Life-cycle Status

The 'cash cows'   These are the products that serve a mature but not yet declining market. Normally, the point has been passed where a lot of effort is needed to improve the benefits to the customer. The product technology and production engineering have reached stability and there is a relatively low call on overhead support to maintain present production and sales volume.

Selling prices should be above average, and this in conjunction with the lower call on overhead support should make this product a cash generator, hence the term 'cash cow'.

If you have too high a market share, there is still a threat from a smaller competitor trying to muscle in. Equally, if you have too low a market share, you may be the first to be squeezed out when the market declines. But provided your market share is neither too high nor too low then this is a product that can potentially generate the cash to support your entry into newer growth markets.

The 'stars'   These are the products at the start of their product life-cycle. Innovation often features prominently in the development of a 'star' product. The early phase of the market development requires above-average marketing know-how and high development costs. The gross margins are above average, but the break-even point may not be reached until some time has elapsed. Also, the cumulative costs of product development and marketing mean that the product will be a net consumer of cash for quite some way into the growth stage of its life-cycle.

Such a product may represent the future success of the business, but it will require substantial funding over its early life-cycle. A 'cash cow' is therefore a perfect counterbalance for a 'star'.

Success Models for Loss-making Companies

The successful models for moving from loss to profit include most of the following:

- Concentrate on reducing costs rather than on increasing sales. Trying to grow out of trouble carries a high risk and is likely to involve unforeseen increases in the cost structure, especially in marketing costs. Look instead for ways to raise production efficiency, for low-cost improvements in production engineering and for reductions in quality costs.
- Find every affordable means of improving customer benefits, especially in the areas of product quality and delivery performance. This can lead quickly to increases in both sales volume and selling price.
- Concentrate on the core business. If necessary, eliminate upstream component manufacturing and contract to the core production process or final assembly where the real value is added to the product. Minimize the involvement in downstream distribution, especially if there is a high call on working capital to finance inventories.
- Avoid all unnecessary risks. You do not have the financial strength to do so. The greatest risks come from moving into new products, new markets or new technologies.
- Become more selective. Concentrate on niche markets where a higher added value can be obtained. Withdraw from undifferentiated market sectors that are dominated by larger and profitable competitors. Above all, do not diversify.
- Cut out significant expenditure that is related to tomorrow rather than today. You may regret it later, but you may at least still be alive to regret it. If necessary mothball the 'star' products until you have turned the corner.
- Make sure the organization is highly motivated towards that

one key objective of getting out of the red. You need above-average management and your routes to the market need to be especially well tuned.

- If the problem is a structural one, cut out the cancer as quickly as possible. Restructuring onto a lower fixed cost base with a lower sales volume of higher margin products is the most certain model for success.

14

The key to restructuring

Restructuring implies a contraction of the business from its present size and form. That will comprise:

- Selective withdrawal from less profitable market sectors. This also implies a reduction in the total gross margin generated.
- Retention of a reduced number of market sectors with above-average profitability.
- Reduction of the cost structure to the minimum level needed to support only the market sectors being retained.

It follows that the reductions in the cost base must exceed the reductions in gross margins by at least the amount of the present loss.

Of all the headings presented on the strategic compass in Chapter 8 this is the most painful one to follow. Before the restructuring is completed many old friends—customers as well as employees—will no longer be with you. The only thing to do is to bite the bullet and get on with it as swiftly and as painlessly as possible.

In Chapter 12 we noted that this course of action has a high chance of success. That is true only if it is done correctly. There are many examples of companies that have restructured, only to find that the losses remain. The reason for this is usually that they have concentrated primarily on reducing costs without having first determined what the new shape of the business should be. We shall avoid such a danger by following a very logical planning framework.

THE PLANNING FRAMEWORK

The framework we shall follow comprises the following steps:

- Business profile. We shall consider first what the business profile should be like in the future. The key to this will be to examine people productivity and product profitability in more depth. Within both of these a mathematical distribution will exist which, if understood properly, will enable you to select a combination of people and products that should be the foundation for a healthy business.
- 'Try for fit'. Then we shall use an approximation, or 'try for fit' calculation, to see if a break-even may be possible with this business profile and within the existing fixed cost structure. It may not, and so at that point we must consider how the fixed cost base could be reduced.
- Zero-base budget. Once the issue of the fixed cost base has been resolved, we shall then be in a position to make a new budget for the company. Instead of starting from the present position and seeking cost reductions, we shall start from a zero-base position and budget only for the costs actually necessary to support the new business profile. In the process we shall prepare 'mini-budgets' for each product group. As we consolidate these one by one into the overall budget, we shall find the best possible plan for the future.
- Costs of restructuring. We shall then calculate the costs that will be directly incurred as a result of the restructuring process.
- Implementation. Finally we shall consider in more detail how an extremely sensitive plan such as this may be implemented successfully.

A NEW BUSINESS PROFILE

A new and healthy business profile will be found by a combination of:

- The most productive part of the people resources
- The most profitable part of the product mix

Before making any predictions about what may be possible, let us see what we might expect if we look in depth at both people productivity and product profitability.

Productivity—a Normal Distribution

Let us first consider the direct workforce, the people who make the products. They are the key to the part of productivity that is controllable. Some of the direct staff will be seen to be more productive than others. You may not be able to measure this precisely, but as you move around the shopfloor you will notice some whose work-rate is above average, who make fewer mistakes and who always finish the job rather than downing tools at the end of the day.

At the opposite extreme will be quite a few whose output is below par, whose hearts and minds are not really in their work and who probably account for a substantial percentage of the total rejects.

Suppose you were able to put a measurement of productivity against each and every member of the direct labour force, for example, by expressing their performance as a percentage of standard times or standard output. Or if there are no standards, by asking the production manager to do it on a basis of 'gut-feel'.

If you plot these individual productivity measurements on a graph, you should find that the graph follows something approaching a normal distribution, as shown in Fig. 14.1.

What this distribution means in very approximate terms is:

- The more productive half of the staff do very nearly 60 per cent of the total work.

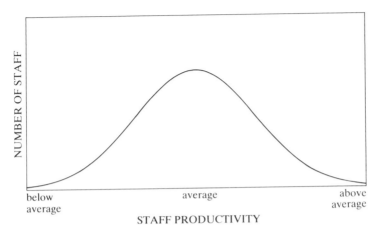

Figure 14.1   Normal distribution

- The best two-thirds do three-quarters of the work.

In reality there is quite likely to be a tail skewing off towards the left-hand side of this graph for two reasons:

- There is a very finite upper limit to how well the really good employee can perform and, sustained over a long period, it is not going to be much more than about one-third above standard.
- The only finite lower limit is zero. Towards the left-hand side of the graph lie not just the slower workers but also a disproportionate part of the quality costs. The people whose minds are not on their work make the most mistakes.

If we take this into account, then what it really implies is:

- The better half of the direct labour force will produce nearer to two-thirds of the *non-rejectable* production.
- The best two-thirds will account for almost 80 per cent.

Profitability—the Rule of Thirds
Now let us examine product profitability. The more detailed the breakdown by product is, the more beneficial this analysis will be.

It could be useful, for example, to consider product profitability at the level of product and customer.

Take a sheet of paper and divide it into columns with the following headings:

- Product or product group
- Gross margin per pound direct labour cost
- Gross margin, total (£)
- Cumulative gross margin (£)
- Cumulative gross margin (%)
- Sales value (£)
- Cumulative sales value (£)
- Cumulative sales value (%)

Then prepare an analysis using the following steps:

- List the products in descending order of gross margin per pound of direct labour cost.
- Against each product enter the total pounds gross margin and the pounds sales value.
- Work down the cumulative gross margin column, calculating the cumulative gross margin at each line on the list. The cumulative figure is the total of that product and all the products above it on the list.
- Do the same for sales value. In both columns the last cumulative figure is also the grand total for all the products.
- Now work down the two percentage columns calculating the cumulative value at each line as a percentage of the grand total.
- Finally, draw a line across the page as near as you can to where the cumulative sales value percentage is 33 per cent, and also to where it is 67 per cent.

You should find that the 'rule of thirds' applies:

- The top third of the total sales value should account for roughly 50 per cent of the total gross margin.
- The middle third will be about a third of total gross margin.
- The bottom third should be in the region of 15–20 per cent.

What this really means is:

- About half the total gross margin is being generated by about one-third of the production effort.
- Eighty per cent or more will be being generated by about two-thirds of that effort.

The Key to Restructuring

We have now established two very interesting statistics:

- Half of the direct staff accounts for about two-thirds of the productive effort.
- Two-thirds of the effort accounts for about 80 per cent of the total gross margin.

Take these two together and it means:

- Half the staff are capable of generating 80 per cent of the total gross margin.

It may seem too good to be true, but it is supportable and predictable by the application of 'A' level mathematics. What is more, it normally will be found in practice to be true.

Understanding this gives you a golden key to a restructuring programme.

It does *not* mean that half the direct labour costs will support 80 per cent of the gross margin. That half of the staff who are the most productive will almost certainly also be the more highly paid, and you must now do some calculations based on individual rates of pay so as to establish the relationship between the wage costs and the gross margin.

That will whittle back some of the potential benefit. It may mean that half the direct labour costs could sustain not 80 per cent of gross margin, but perhaps something nearer to only two-thirds instead. But there are some advantages to compensate for this:

- Hidden costs will reduce greatly. There will be fewer mistakes made, the product quality will improve, the quality costs will reduce and the whole factory will work more smoothly. The customer service will in turn improve.

- Customer benefits will be enhanced as a result and that will enhance your competitive position. You may even be able to get more business for those products that have the above-average gross margin, or you may be able to get a higher margin because the customers will be prepared to pay more for the greater benefit now offered to them.

The great temptation at this stage is to decide which products are going to be discontinued and which staff should be made redundant, and then get the restructuring programme down in black and white and into action as quickly as possible. The framework we established at the start of this chapter will produce a very much better way of doing it than that.

A 'TRY FOR FIT' CALCULATION

Before going any further we need to know whether that key to restructuring will in fact lead the company back to profit. There is a quick way of establishing this. We shall do an approximation or a 'try for fit' type of exercise. Once again a spreadsheet will make this much easier. The steps are as follows:

- Start with the most recent set of management accounts and the latest analysis of costs, split between those that are controllable and those that are not controllable, like the rent and rates.
- Extrapolate these accounts into the equivalent annualized figures, taking account of any seasonal factors and anything finite that is known about the future.
- Do a series of 'what if?' calculations, starting from the annualized projection of the current results.
- Substitute the more favourable combination of direct labour costs and gross margin which has emerged as the key to restructuring.

- Amend sales revenue and material costs to match up with the products included in that combination.
- Assume that overhead staff numbers and wage costs will reduce pro rata to the reductions in direct labour.
- Assume that each controllable but non-wage overhead cost reduces pro rata to the key factor which drives it. For example, in the case of shipping costs it could be sales volume, and in the case of telephone costs it could be the number of overhead staff. For the moment this need only be a 'ball-park' estimate.
- Leave uncontrollable fixed costs unchanged in this 'what if?' calculation.

Now what does the bottom-line look like? If it is in the black, or very close to it, then the business can support the existing fixed cost structure and we can now go ahead and prepare a new budget.

But if the bottom-line still shows a loss, then you must first consider how to lower the uncontrollable fixed costs. We shall need the answer to that before preparing a new budget.

A Lower Fixed Cost Structure

The key to reducing the uncontrollable fixed cost structure will vary from company to company. Very often, however, the highest uncontrollable fixed cost will be rent and rates. In that case you must consider either of these options:

- Sub-letting part of the existing premises
- Relocation to smaller and less costly premises

If the reason for the high cost is not excessive space but excessive rental levels, it may be necessary to relocate to a more distant area where lower rents prevail.

Relocation will present its own problems:

- How to retain key staff
- High costs of relocation
- Disruption to the business.

These must be considered in depth before any decision is made.

At this stage you will most probably not have numbers finite enough to help select an alternative lower fixed cost option which fits properly with the detailed budget we are about to prepare. The most helpful approach will be to identify a set of options that looks feasible but that would cater for a range of different sizes of business. As we prepare the budget we shall begin by using the least-cost option and then substitute higher-cost options if and when they are needed.

THE ZERO-BASE BUDGET

The technique we shall use to prepare a new budget for the company is 'zero-base budgeting'. We shall start with a clean sheet of paper and build the plan up from a zero-base position. That will force us to justify every product being retained and not just the products being discarded. It will force us to justify the costs being incurred rather than the savings we can make. It will be much more positive and it will enable us to find the best possible plan.

This new budget will be prepared in a number of stages:

- Zero base. We start from a zero position. There are no costs and no sales. The bottom-line shows zero profit and zero loss.
- Unavoidable fixed costs. We shall then insert only the un-avoidable fixed costs, the costs you must incur *before* produc-ing even one unit of product. At this stage the bottom-line will show a large loss.
- Product group 'mini-budgets'. Then we shall take your prod-uct groups one at a time, and in a particular order, and add the sales of these products into this plan, working out as we do what additional costs will be needed to support just this incremental addition to production and sales.

Each time we do this the bottom-line loss will begin to reduce. We should finally reach break-even and after that move to a position of profit. We shall keep adding in more of your product lines until we reach a point where doing so would not improve the bottom-line result. At that point the law of diminishing returns will be taking hold; stopping just short of that will give:

- The best possible restructuring plan

We shall now prepare a zero-base budget, using data from a case study to add an element of realism to the exercise. Yet again the use of a spreadsheet will make this task much easier. The format of this budget will be similar to the one shown in Table 14.1, but

Table 14.1   Zero base budget (£000)

	Base	*A*	*B*	*C*	*D*	*E*	*F*
A. *Mini-budgets*							
Sales revenue	0	0	495	421	475	217	373
Material costs	0	0	146	159	161	73	208
Direct labour	0	0	78	77	137	55	63
Gross margin	0	0	271	185	177	89	102
Overhead costs							
people costs	0	79	0	70	91	46	85
other costs	0	165	46	79	74	39	82
Total overheads	0	244	46	149	165	85	167
Profit/(loss)	0	(244)	225	36	12	4	(65)
B. *Consolidated budget*							
Sales revenue	0	0	495	916	1391	1608	1981
Material costs	0	0	146	305	466	539	747
Direct labour	0	0	78	155	292	347	410
Gross margin	0	0	271	456	633	722	824
Overhead costs							
people costs	0	79	79	149	240	286	371
other costs	0	165	211	290	364	403	485
Total overheads	0	244	290	439	604	689	856
Profit/(loss)	0	(244)	(19)	17	29	33	(32)

you must allow for building up the detail of each column step by step.

Case Study—Company X

The current position of company X is:

- Annual sales: £2.5 million
- Annual loss: £450 000.

The company has identified six product groups (B, C, D, E, F and G). An analysis of product profitability is shown in Table 14.2. In this example these were the actual product groups shown in Fig. 12.4 (page 176).

The strategic position of these groups is as follows:

- Product group B is a 'cash cow'; the market is mature, but may be expected to decline a few years along the way.

If you have any 'cash cow' products, this is an appropriate time to visit the key customers for these products. Ask them what their future plans are. If they are large companies, they may well have a strategic plan of their own and may be able to give you the key to the expected future life of this product group. That information will be vital when preparing this new budget.

Table 14.2   Product profitability analysis

Product group	Sales £000	Gross margin £000	Gross margin %
B	495	271	54.7
C	421	185	43.9
D	475	177	37.3
E	217	89	41.0
F	373	102	27.3
G	519	(26)	negative

- Product group E: the market is growing rapidly as a result of product substitution. The company is a relative newcomer to this market and gross margins are expected to improve as the company grows out of the learning curve. This is a 'star' product.

The markets for the remaining product groups are all relatively attractive, but the company cost structure is not competitive. To correct this would mean replacing the core production equipment and installing the more automated technology that the major competitors already have. That would cost £500 000.

Within these remaining markets there are four distinct sectors:

- Product group C: this is a speciality product serving a clearly defined niche within the market; the cost structure may not be attractive, but this is outweighed by the more competitive benefits the company offers its customers.
- Product group D: company X lacks the benefit of a superior product, but this sector comprises many small-volume customers who are not price-sensitive. This sector is not as attractive to competitors, whose more automated technology has made them more volume-oriented. The cost structure is therefore competitive, and the customers benefit from company X's ability to produce small runs.
- Product group G: this is serving the high-volume price-sensitive end of the same market as product group D. The company's backward production technology makes it completely uncompetitive; taking business at market price levels results in a negative gross margin.
- Product group F: between the low-volume end of the market and the price-sensitive end is a grey area in the middle where there is an undifferentiated product and a relatively uncompetitive cost structure. The relatively low gross margins reflect this.

There are two decisions which can now be made before starting to prepare a new budget:

- Eliminate product group G. Any product with a negative margin cannot possibly lead the company back to profit. The wisdom of retaining product group F is also in doubt. In most manufacturing businesses it is likely only to be the products with gross margins approaching 40 per cent or more that will ensure a viable future. In this example it will quite simply depend on how important product group F's total gross margin of £K102 is to the recovery of the unavoidable fixed costs, and we do not yet know this.
- Do *not* spend that £500 000 on new production equipment, at least not in the immediate future. The right time to think about spending that money is *after* the restructuring plan has been implemented and has demonstrated that there is then a viable business that will justify the investment of that new money.

Unavoidable Fixed Costs

The first step in the budget exercise is to calculate the unavoidable fixed costs simply of being in business. These are the costs the company must incur before it produces one unit of product. These costs will include:

- Rent and rates on the smallest module of premises that can be retained or to which the company can relocate.
- Associated overhead costs, like lighting and heating the building. For the moment ignore all the other works overhead costs. We shall take account of these only as and when we decide which product groups should be added into the budget.
- Costs of the minimum number of people who between them can perform every job in the company. How many people would you really need if you were prepared to run the business 'off the back of a postage stamp'?
- Unavoidable costs of administration. This will include the very minimum cost necessary to remain open to receive orders. It need not include any selling costs, but it will

certainly include the costs of having the telephone and fax lines open, and providing other basic items of office equipment.

These costs should be added up and entered in column A of Table 14.1.

Product Group Mini-budgets

The next step is to take the various product groups, one by one, and prepare 'mini-budgets' for each one. The order in which we do this is very important. The fastest way to make a dent in the unavoidable costs is to take the product group with the greatest total gross margin. This however takes no account of any variation in the rate at which the different products attract overhead costs.

The correct sequence will be as follows:

- 'Cash cows'. Take the 'cash cows' first, provided they at least account for a substantial amount of gross margin. These will have relatively low demands on many overhead cost elements. In Table 14.2 this was product B.
- Products that generate a large total gross margin *and* have above-average percentage margins. In our example this was product group C.
- Products that have only an above-average percentage margin. Product group E fell in this category.
- Products that have only a large total margin. This included product groups D and F.

For each product group in turn we shall now prepare a mini-budget. The numbers we need to estimate are these:

- Sales revenue: we shall assume unchanged sales, unless we are certain of any reason why that will not be valid.
- Material costs: we know the material cost percentage from the product profitability analysis and so we can calculate material cost of sales as a percentage of sales revenue.

- Direct labour costs: calculation of this is very important. The product costing systems must provide sufficient data to allow us to work out just how many people will be needed to achieve this production. We will ignore the previous department structure and instead think more simply in terms of the broad categories of skills needed. Work out how many people will be needed in each skill category, making allowance for down-time, sickness and holidays.

  Now put names to them, selecting first the most productive people, the most flexible and those with multiple skills. Their rates of pay are known, so we can now calculate the direct labour costs. Before finishing, work out how much unused capacity remains in each skill area that can be used to support some production of another product group.

- Overhead costs: we shall split these quite simply into two categories—people costs and other costs:

  – People costs. For the very first product group you include, you will not need very much of a management structure. The business can still be run off the back of an envelope. There are many tasks, which you currently employ people to do, that can be done by that core group of unavoidable staff listed under column A. You should find that you need surprisingly few overhead staff to begin with.

    As we move along and include a few more product groups the overhead structure will grow. You will begin to need some form of management structure. You will need to start inserting some of the more specific overhead functions, like production control, quality control, purchasing, a stores foreman, and so on. The number of administration staff will expand as well. You may need an accountant, as well as some dedicated sales administration staff.

    In Table 14.1 this growth in the overhead structure took place when product group C was inserted into the budget. If we were to project forward to a business several times the size of that in Table 14.1, there would come a point where these additional overhead staff would expand into whole departments and that would need another layer of management as well.

As regards sales staff, this budget is not about growing sales, it is simply about maintaining sales of selected products. Which of these tasks is the existing sales team employed to do? You should certainly not need field sales staff to maintain your 'cash cow' business; you can perhaps spend a couple of days a month attending to this yourself. As you insert a few more product groups you may very well need someone just to perform the 'service salesman' job.

– Other costs. With each product group you will start to make use of production equipment; this will involve power costs, maintenance and depreciation. You may even reach a point where you need additional modules of factory space. There will be distribution costs, and there will be some part of most of the cost elements which presently appear on the detailed analyses attached to your management accounts.

We must ask just how much of these variable costs will be necessary to support this one product group. There may be some items where we can do nothing but take the current on-going cost, and split that pro rata to sales volume, numbers employed or whatever yardstick is most relevant.

• Action plans. Before you finish with each product group, go back to the company audits carried out in Chapter 11, when we analysed the company in some depth. Are there any low-cost and low-effort action plans you could reasonably include in each of these mini-budgets? If there are, then include them in the mini-budget. Write them down, take account of any improvement this would make to any of the figures and make a memo note of any once-off costs that would be associated with this action.

You may not be able to put these action plans into effect on day 1 of the restructuring, but by the second or third month you should certainly find that you have the time and effort to do so, and you may need a further challenge by that time.

The Consolidated Budget

To complete the zero base budget we take all of these mini-budgets in turn and insert them onto the format shown in Table 14.1. We then calculate the cumulative effect as we go from left to right across the page. If we have selected the product groups in the right sequence, then we shall find a picture similar to the one shown in Table 14.1. The benefit of adding in additional product groups first improves, and then starts to lessen as we move to the right.

Looking at that particular example you may well think that anything included after product group B is not giving nearly as much return for the additional effort. If the numbers were only slightly different, such that product group B alone would produce a bottom-line profit, you may think very carefully about whether or not you should settle for just that one product group alone.

But remember that this first product group was the 'cash cow'. The market will decline at some stage in the not too distant future. If you put all your eggs in this one basket, the future of the business may vanish when that market declines. That is a high risk to take. You need some other products to guarantee a future, and you will have plenty of time ahead of you to grow the sales of these before the 'cash cows' run dry of milk. In the meantime be thankful that this product will help pay for such a large part of the fixed costs and so give you more time to solve the problems of the future.

Remember also that in the case study we used the cost structure was not competitive. Once this company is back in profit it may be able to justify that major new investment which will put this right. After that there may be less of a disparity in terms of reward for effort as we move along Table 14.1 through product groups C and D.

The Best Possible Plan

For the moment the question is: What is the best possible plan? Looking at the bottom-line numbers in Table 14.1, it is not very obvious. We must clearly include product group C as well as product group B, and we will certainly stop short of including product group F. In between lies a greyer area. Do we include product groups D and E, or not?

This is where we must exercise some judgement based on previous analysis:

- If the markets for these products are attractive, and if there is a possibility of gaining a competitive position in the medium-term future, then we shall include them. In the example we have just used the competitive position could well improve if, once back in the black, company X were able to justify that capital investment in new production technology.
- If the market is unattractive, or if we cannot foresee the company occupying a competitive position, then we shall discard these products from the new budget.

Having exercised judgement in this way to temper the bald numbers, we shall then have arrived at the best possible plan.

In front of you now on a sheet of paper is the budget you will be working to *after* you have carried out the necessary restructuring. You know what product groups you are going to continue to make and sell, and you have a list of the people you are going to continue to employ.

There are two more things to do:

- Calculate restructuring costs.
- Implement the plan.

COSTS OF RESTRUCTURING

The costs of restructuring will include the following:

- Redundancy costs: you have a list of the staff you will retain. You will make the rest redundant. The costs will include redundancy pay, and pay in lieu of notice, plus holiday pay in respect of holiday entitlement not used up.
- Write-off of assets: as you completed the product group

mini-budgets you identified the production equipment and other assets you need to run the business in its new shape. Anything else you have but do not need should be disposed of. Do not clutter up the place with redundant equipment. This applies just as much in the offices as on the shopfloor. The write-off will be the difference between book value and the proceeds of disposal. If any of the equipment is leased, then you will also have the penalty costs of terminating these leases.

- Write-off of stock: if you have stock that is specific to any of the product groups being eliminated, you will have to write off the difference between book value and the estimated proceeds of sale.

- Physical costs of restructuring: you will most likely be moving plant and equipment out as you withdraw from some product groups. You should also take advantage of this to make any improvements you can to the plant layout at the same time. Moving things around costs money. You may need sub-contractors to do the moving or to disconnect and reconnect plant, and you may need some additional insurance cover while it is all taking place.

- Costs of relocation: you may have substantial costs of relocation, if that is also part of the plan; this needs very detailed budgeting.

- Cost of action plans: finally, you may have the much smaller costs of the action plans for improvement that you included in the product group mini-budgets.

The total costs of this restructuring plan will no doubt be a quite staggering figure. You can calculate the pay-back period by comparing the total costs to the turn round in the bottom-line result. For example, in the case of company X (Table 14.1), the bottom-line turn round would be in the region of £467–483 000, depending on which product groups were retained. If the costs of restructuring were £240 000—a quite probable figure—this still gives a pay-back of only six months. It would be a good investment to make. Outright closure would probably cost twice as much; while doing nothing would lead to bankruptcy.

IMPLEMENTATION

The remaining task is to make it all happen and, as always, this is both the most important and the most difficult step. As with the survival plan (Chapter 6) there is a need for professional project management. This restructuring plan has an additional element which makes it different from most other plans. Because of the effect it will have on a large number of employees and on many customers it is much more *sensitive* and so requires special attention. Some elements must be handled very carefully. We shall consider them under four headings:

- Detailed planning stage. There are some items that must be planned in detail before the restructuring plan is put into effect.
- The human relations aspect. In making staff redundant you will inevitably cause pain and suffering. No matter how stretched your resources may be, take the time to find every possible means of helping them through this trauma.
- Action on the day. The action taken on the day the plan is put into effect is extremely critical to the success of the plan.
- Production considerations. It will be important to prevent production arrears following in the wake of a redundancy programme. There is also a once-off possibility of improving the production layout.

Detailed Planning Stage

As soon as the basic restructuring plan is agreed, get down to some very detailed planning at a nuts and bolts level. This is a plan which must, and can, be executed without hitches. The most important features are these ones:

Confidentiality Keep the plan confidential within a limited trusted circle at this stage. You cannot carry it out on your own, but it must be known to others strictly on a 'need-to-know' rather than a 'nice-to-know' basis.

Consultation   The position may be complicated if you have a legal obligation to consult with a trade union. If you do, your plan will not remain confidential and your choice of which employees to retain and which to dismiss may be subject to any agreements that are in force. As soon as the possibility of redundancy becomes known it is likely to be the best staff who will thwart your plans by finding alternative jobs. This is a potential major problem which you must address in the light of the specific circumstances within your company.

Timing   Choose the earliest possible date for implementing the redundancy programme. The lead-time will be limited to the time it takes to prepare redundancy pay and to conform to any obligations you may have to notify the Department of Employment (DoE).

Notification   Your solicitor will advise you as to what these obligations may be. When you complete the form of notification to the DoE, avoid using the company address for return correspondence. Instead, use your home address, or that of a parent group or solicitor. Send the return to a regional office of the DoE and not to the local office. These precautions may help prevent news of the plans accidentally leaking out. Also, study carefully the grounds you may have for implementing the redundancies before the legal period of notice has expired.

Selection for redundancy   Keep in mind the fact that you are selecting staff to retain and not the staff to dismiss. If you stick to the principle of last-in first-out, you will sacrifice a large part of the key to restructuring we saw earlier in this chapter. Do not be influenced by how much redundancy pay any specific person may be entitled to. Rather, make sure you retain the very best members of your workforce, even if it costs more to make the others redundant.

Justification   Be prepared to justify the basis for selecting those being made redundant, in case you later face an unfair dismissal claim. In law it is jobs you are making redundant, not individuals. The question of selection arises when you have fewer of the same jobs available in future as you had in the past.

The most supportable basis for selection for redundancy may be that in the smaller restructured company you will require people with multiple skills to provide greater work flexibility. You may also decide to eliminate a whole layer of the organization structure. Having the right staff in the appropriate job categories before you start can be a big advantage.

Have a written statement, made in advance, of the basis for selection. This should cover every job being made redundant. Keep it under lock and key until you need it.

Period of notice   Plan to implement the redundancies without notice and give pay in lieu of notice. Do not make anyone work out the period of notice that they are entitled to under their contract of employment. That will only sap the morale of the staff you wish to retain.

Redundancy pay   For each person being made redundant, make sure you have prepared the following items in advance:

- A letter notifying them of the redundancy.
- A statement showing the calculation of redundancy pay and pay in lieu of notice; a cheque for this amount. These items are tax-free and can be prepared in advance. Outstanding pay to the date of termination may have to wait until you next run the payroll, and you can post this to them along with a P45. Ensure you know everyone's present home address.

The Human Relations Aspect
Many of the staff being made redundant will have given years of

service to the company. Even where their performance has not been especially high, most will nevertheless have worked conscientiously and to the best of their abilities. They deserve some consideration at this unfortunate moment in their career.

Your treatment of these staff must be based on a combination of:

- Fact: there is no escaping the need for the redundancies, but there will be less ill-feeling if the facts are presented clearly.
- Legality: this has been covered under the heading of preplanning.
- Humanity: give maximum consideration to the staff being made redundant.

Among the actions you can take to make this experience less painful are these:

- A reference. Have written references ready to give them to help in their task of finding another job. Do not wait to be asked for the reference. Give this to them along with their notice of redundancy and redundancy payment.
- Additional compensation. Your legal obligation in terms of redundancy pay is clear. It is also fairly meagre. If you possibly can, make additional payments in excess of the legal minimum entitlement, especially in the case of long-serving or older employees who may have greater difficulty in finding alternative employment.
- Give help where needed in preparing CVs.
- Consider offering career counselling at the company's expense.
- Give them help in their task of seeking a new job, for example by circulating details of those made redundant to other companies in the vicinity or in the same industry.

This additional help can be offered either in the letter of notification of redundancy, in a follow-up letter to each ex-employee, or even by verbal contact on the part of departmental or personnel management.

Action on the Day

Timing and coordination   Make sure this part of your plan goes like clock-work. Avoid doing it on a Monday or a Friday. Do it in the morning, just before lunch. Get together all those being made redundant, give them the sad news, give them their letters and pay, and see them off the site as quickly as possible. Then spend a lot of time with the remaining staff explaining to them as carefully as you can why this has been done and what the results are going to be in a few months' time. Emphasize the mid- to long-term prospects.

All of this will need a careful timetable and meticulous planning. You cannot be with everyone at the same time, so you will need a lot of concerted action by a handful of key managers to make it work without hitch.

Notifying customers   On that same day, and not before, notify your customers and suppliers. If you do not do it, the grapevine will do it for you. You must ensure that your customers hear your side of the story first. Accentuate the positive. Tell them what you are going to do in the future, not what you are giving up. It helps retain credibility if you can give reasons other than the need to stop the losses.

Production Considerations

From a production point of view you should take account of the following factors:

Avoid production arrears   Well before the implementation date make sure you work all the overtime you possibly can, with the sole objective of producing as far forward into the works order book as is possible. When a large number of staff leave at once you will be in a stronger position if production is many weeks in advance of due completion date. That will provide a buffer which should ensure that no customer will be let down as a result of the sudden action.

There may also be a time-lag while you disengage from the business you are discarding, and in between you may have a higher order book than the reduced staff levels can cope with. The very last thing you need at this critical point is to get into arrears with production.

Timing of physical restructuring Plan the remaining part of the restructuring plan, the physical movement of plant and equipment, or relocation, to coincide with the next major holiday or works shut-down. In the interval the production environment may be less than perfect, but you cannot afford to lose valuable production time. It is better to do it over New Year, Easter or a bank holiday, when many customers will also be closed. You can always extend the shut-down by a few days either side if you need it.

Revised layout Take the maximum advantage you possibly can of planning this physical restructuring so as to give a better factory layout than you had before. It is a golden opportunity which may not present itself again for a long time to come.

Appendix 1

Sources of help and advice

BIBLIOGRAPHY

The following are sound, readable and well-signposted introductions to the major aspects of management:

Warnes, B., *The Genghis Khan Guide to Business*, Osmosis, London, 1984.

Bull, R. J., *Accounting in Business*, Butterworth, London, 1990.

Baker, M. J. (ed.), *The Marketing Book*, Institute of Marketing/Heinemann, London, 1987.

Allen, P., *Selling: Management and Practice*, M+E Handbooks, London, 1973.

Attwood, M., *Personnel Management*, Macmillan, London, 1985.

Price, F., *Right First Time*, Gower, Aldershot, 1985.

Prabhu, V. and M. Baker, *Production Management and Control*, IPC/McGraw-Hill, Maidenhead, 1986.

GENERAL SOURCES OF HELP

The following should offer initial help and a 'gateway' to more specific help:

- Bank Manager: most banks have a business manager at regional level; ask your bank manager for an introduction.
- Accountants or Auditors: they may also be able to offer consultancy and recruitment services.
- Trade Associations: if you belong to one.

- Enterprise Agencies: these are partnerships between local companies and local authorities and are staffed by managers from the participating firms. There are about 300 agencies across the United Kingdom. Informal discussions are free of charge and there is no limit to how often you may use the service. Use them as a 'sounding board' for advice of a general nature. They have no funding for anything else.

    Your local enterprise agency will be listed in the local telephone directory under your county or city (e.g. Berkshire Enterprise Agency). Alternatively, dial 100 and ask for Freefone Enterprise.

    Small Firms Service: this is operated by the Department of Employment. It is most useful purely as a source of information, but the service also extends to advice from professionals (e.g. accountants, solicitors, etc.). This service is normally provided by retired professionals operating on a part-time basis. Up to three sessions can be provided free of charge. To contact your local office dial 100 and ask for Freefone Enterprise.

- Training and Enterprise Councils (TECs): there are approximately 30 of these councils operating on a regional basis. At the time of writing these were just being set up. The service will be all-embracing and will have government funding which may be used to help you. The administration will be handled by local business people. To contact your regional TEC dial 100 and ask for Freefone Enterprise.

- Chamber of Commerce: many will have extensive reference libraries and import/export documentation services. If you need help to locate your local chamber, contact:

    Association of British Chambers of Commerce
    Sovereign House
    212A Shaftesbury Avenue
    London WC2H 8EW
    Tel: 071-240 5831

- Department of Trade and Industry: the publication *A Guide for Business* lists the services of the DTI under the following headings:
  - Regional network
  - Market contacts
  - Policies, functions and support services

The gateway to DTI services is through your local office or at the address below. The DTI is listed in telephone directories as: 'Trade and Industry Department of':

DTI (Dept 2d)
Freepost
London SW1V 1YX
Tel: 0800-500 200

MANAGEMENT CONSULTANTS

The following sources can be used to identify management consultants or consultancy help:

- *Directory of Management Consultants in the UK:* the most complete list of management consultancy practices, cross-indexed by:
  - Areas of specialization
  - Industry specialization
  - Geographical area

  Available in most reference libraries and is published by:

  TFPL Publishing
  22 Peter's Lane
  London EC1M 6DS
  Tel: 071-251 5522

- Institute of Management Consultants: the consultants' own professional association:

Institute of Management Consultants
5th Floor
32–33 Hatton Garden
London EC1N 8DL
Tel: 071-242 2140

- University/Technical College Business Studies Departments: some will seek consultancy assignments for business studies students; others provide a fully-fledged consultancy service.

- Enterprise Initiative: the Consultancy Initiatives of the DTI's Enterprise Initiative programme provide subsidized consultancy to companies with fewer than 500 employees, provided they are not part of a parent group employing more than 2500 employees. Up to 15 man-days consultancy is available, with a subsidy of 50 per cent of the fees (or two-thirds in assisted areas of the United Kingdom). This assistance can be provided for two separate projects. The DTI imposes a ceiling on the consultancy fees, and this is lower than the normal rate charged by many consultancy practices.

  Consultancy Initiatives include the following:

  – Marketing
  – Design
  – Quality
  – Manufacturing
  – Business planning
  – Financial and information systems

  The programmes are managed on behalf of the DTI by external organizations (Institute of Marketing, 3i Enterprise Support Ltd and PERA). The initial contact point is your local office of the DTI.

- Training Agency: subsidized consultancy is also available from the state-funded Training Agency. The main objective is provision of training, including management training. There are four options, one of which is geared to the management of change and could include planning for turn round as recommended in this book. The restrictions are also less inhibiting than those of the Enterprise Initiative programme. Contact is:

Business Growth Training
Freepost (TK 450)
Brentford
Middx TW8 8BR
Tel: 0800-300 787

- Executive Leasing: consider this as an alternative to consultancy. You could lease an executive with experience of managing a turn-round situation. Possible contacts are:

The Executive Register Ltd	Tel: (071) 387 9291
Ernst & Young	Tel: (071) 495 7808
Executive Stand-by Ltd	Tel: (0606) 883849
GMS Executive Leasing	Tel: (0582) 666970

INFORMATION TECHNOLOGY

For an appreciation of the business use of computers and personal computers, spreadsheets, database languages and accounting packages consider the following:

- Local Education Authority: adult studies programmes at local schools or colleges may include these subjects and will normally be advertised in local papers before the start of each term.
- *Sunday Times* Video Series: a series of 12 videos specifically for business users. For details contact:

Taylor Made Distribution Ltd
Harrington Dock
Liverpool X, L70 1AX
Tel: 051-708 8202

MARKETING STRATEGY

As an introduction to marketing strategy, short management courses are available. Contacts include the following:

The Institute of Marketing
Moor Hall
Cookham
Berks SL6 9QH
Tel: 06285 24922

Cranfield School of Management
Cranfield
Bedford MK43 0AL
Tel: 0234 751122

MARKET RESEARCH

General Sources of Data

The most comprehensive sources of marketing information will be found in reference libraries or in on-line marketing databases. Both should contain much of the data listed under the more specific headings which follow.

- City Business Library, City Wall, London (until the end of 1991 located in Fenchurch Street). Tel: (071) 638 8215. This has an extensive collection of published market data and market research.
- County Libraries: the reference section of county central libraries. The amount and quality of information varies from county to county. This should be the best source of comprehensive, *local* market data. Many county libraries now have information on systems similar to Prestel, which can be accessed free, either in the library or by telephone using a Prestel-type receiver. For more details contact the Director of Information Services of your county library service.
- On-line Marketing Databases: the information contained in on-line marketing databases includes company information,

media extracts and a large amount of market research data. The database is accessed over the public telephone network, using a PC with communications software and a modem or acoustic coupler. For these services there is a registration fee (about £150) plus a charge for the time you are connected to the database (from £1.00 to £1.50 per minute; as this is in addition to the cost of the telephone call itself it is best to select one that allows access via a local telephone number). There are many on-line databases, but most of them will provide a 'gateway' to most others. Two to consider are:

Profile Information
PO Box 12
Sunbury-on-Thames
Middx TW16 7UD
Tel: 0932 761444

Telecom Gold
Tel: 0800-200 700

Industry/Product Classification

To use certain market data you may need to know what classification code applies to your industry or product. These can be found in the following publications:

* Industry code: 'Standard Industrial Classification' (SIC)
* Product code: 'Index of Commodities'

Both are published by:

HMSO
49 High Holborn
London WC1
Tel: 071-211 5656

HMSO also has regional bookshops in Edinburgh, Manchester, Bristol, Birmingham and Belfast.

Identification of Customers/Competitors

The choice falls between making your own list by consulting directories, or buying a selective list from a list broker.

- Trade Directories: to find the right directory, consult *Current British Directories*, which is the directory of trade directories and should be in your local reference library. It is published by:

  CBD Research Ltd
  15 Wickham Road
  Beckenham
  Kent BR3 2JS
  Tel: 081-650 7745

- Classified Business Directories: the most comprehensive will always be those that make no charge for a basic entry. These include:

  Dial Industry Publications
  Windsor Court
  East Grinstead House
  West Sussex RH19 1XA
  Tel: 0342 326972

  who publish separate volumes covering:
  – engineering
  – electrical/electronics
  – computing

- *Business Pages*: seven volumes cover the United Kingdom, but exclude the more rural regions. Available from your local British Telecom office.

- Selective Lists: these can be specified by industry, geographical region, size of company, etc. In many cases, contact names will also be available. Some may cover overseas countries. There is a choice of sources:

Dun & Bradstreet Ltd
Homers Farm Way
High Wycombe, Bucks HP12 4UL
Tel: 0494 422000

Market Location Ltd
17 Waterloo Place
Leamington Spa CV32 5LA
Tel: 0926 34235

The Business Database
Database House
77–83 The Broadway
West Ealing
London W13 9BP
Tel: 081-567 1144

Customer/Competitor Information

- Companies House: The basic source of information is the public records held at Companies House. This includes annual reports and accounts of recent years. Some of the problems associated with this information is discussed in Chapter 10. The records are held on microfiche and can be obtained either by visiting Companies House or by doing a postal search. Microfiche readers are available for public use both at Companies House and at most public libraries. It helps to know the *precise* name of the company being searched, but it is no longer necessary to know the company registration number when requesting a postal search.

  For a search made in person at Companies House the charge is £2.75 per search, but be prepared to wait at least one hour. For a postal search the charge is £5.00 per search, and for a hard copy instead of a microfiche the charge is £6.50 per *document*.

  The location of Companies House depends on a company's country of registration:

England and Wales: Companies House
                                City Road
                                London

But for a postal search: Companies House
                                Crown Way
                                Cardiff CF4 3UZ
                                Tel: 0222 380107

Scotland: Companies House
                                100–102 George Street
                                Edinburgh EH2 3DJ
                                Tel: 031-225 5774

Northern Ireland: Companies Registration Office
                                IDB House
                                Chichester Street
                                Belfast BT1 4JX
                                Tel: 0232 234488

Extensive company information, much of it derived from the public records, can also be obtained from the following sources, who may also have industry-wide and/or regional surveys available on demand:

ICC Information Group Ltd
28–42 Banner Street
London EC1Y 8QE
Tel: 071-253 3906

MBA Market Information Ltd
24 Upper Dicconson Street
Wigan
Lancs WN1 2AG
Tel: 0942 826288

Market Data/Published Market Research
Sources include the following:

DTI Business Statistics Office Tel: 0633 812399

which regularly publishes *Business Monitors*, each of which covers specific groups of products.

Mintel Publications Ltd
18–19 Long Lane
London EC1A 9HE
Tel: 071-606 4533

Mintel publishes both market data and indexes to published market research, with a strong bias towards the retail sector.

Industrial Aids Ltd
14 Buckingham Palace Road
London SW1W 0QP
Tel: 071-828 5036

which publishes volumes relating to different geographical markets.

Marketing Strategies for Industry (UK) Ltd
32 Mill Green Road
Mitcham
Surrey CR4 4HY
Tel: 081-640 6621

which publishes *Marketing Surveys Index*.

EXPORT MARKETS

- The Export Initiative: the services of the DTI are packaged together as 'The Export Initiative'. A brochure is available from the local office of the DTI. The package provides a variety of assistance:

  Export Marketing Consultancy (part of the Enterprise Initiative). The gateway is via your local DTI office.
  European Single Market: the DTI have a special '1992 Hotline': Tel: 081-200 1992.
  Market Research and Intelligence: Many of the services are charged for, and the DTI have now introduced a credit card

for regular users. There are a multitude of entry points to the vast resources available:
Export Market Information Centre, including the BOTIS database:

>DTI Export Market Information Centre
>Victoria Street
>London SW1H 0ET
>Tel: 071-215 8444

The publication *Export Initiative* (page 27) contains a list of direct telephone numbers which can be used for advice on export to specific countries.
Export Market Research Scheme. Contact is:

>The Association of British Chambers of Commerce
>4 Westwood House, Westwood Business Park
>Coventry CV4 8HS
>Tel: 0203 694484

Export Intelligence Service: Any information readily available from the computer databases will normally be provided free of charge, but enquiries requiring research by commercial staff in an overseas embassy will be charged depending on the time taken (up to 4 hours: £50; over 4 hours: £100; plus VAT). Contact:

>DTI
>1 Victoria Street
>London SW1H 0ET
>Tel: 071-215 5000

- Defence Export Services: companies in the defence market may seek export marketing assistance from:

>Defence Export Services Organization
>Room 707, Stuart House
>23–25 Soho Square
>London W1V 5JF
>Tel: 071-632 4826

QUALITY

Useful contacts include:

DTI
Tel: 071-215 6639

BSI Quality Assurance
PO Box 375
Milton Keynes MK14 6LL
Tel: 0908 220908

Yarsley Quality Assured Firms Ltd
Trowers Way
Redhill
Surrey RH1 2JN
Tel: 0737 768445

The latter two addresses will be of especial relevance in the context of BS. 5750 and other quality standards.

PRODUCTION/PROCESS TECHNOLOGY

Sources of help include the following:

DTI
Tel: 071-215 8235

The Engineering Council
Canberra House
Maltravers Street
London WC2R 3ER
Tel: 071-240 7891

Inside UK Enterprise: a scheme sponsored by the DTI which enables companies to visit and learn from more experienced companies. For details contact:

IFS Ltd
Wolsely Business Park
Kempston
Bedford MK42 7PW
Tel: 0234 853605

In addition there are two excellent handbooks available:
Competitive Manufacturing Workbook: this is a guide to a manufacturing audit, published with approval of the DTI, and is available (price £14.95) from:

IFS Ltd
Wolsely Business Park
Kempston
Beds MK42 7PW
Tel: 0234 853605

The Lucas Manufacturing Systems Engineering Handbook: available (price £45) from:

Lucas Engineering & Systems
Sales & Marketing Dept
PO Box 52
Solihull B90 4JJ

PRODUCT TECHNOLOGY/DESIGN

The basic contact points include:

DTI
Tel: 071-215 6989

Design Advisory Service
Design Council
28 Haymarket
London SW1Y 4SU
Tel: 071-839 8000 or 041-221 6121 (Glasgow)

Materials Information Centre: this is a free service set up by the DTI; access is by contacting the Design Centre (see above).

GRANTS AND AIDS

Much of the financial help being made available to business by Government Departments is not being taken up, largely because managers do not know what is available or where to find out what is available. Your bank manager should have a guide to grants and low-cost help. If not, a comprehensive guide (price £35) is available from:

Associated Management Services
10 Broad Street
Swindon SN1 2DR

STAFF REDUNDANCIES

A full information pack can be obtained from the regional offices of the Department of Employment:

Bromley (Kent): Tel: 081-464 6418
Wembley (Middx): Tel: 081-903 1414
Bristol: Tel: 0272 273755
Birmingham: Tel: 021-456 1144
Leeds: Tel: 0532 438232
Manchester: Tel: 061-832 9111
Newcastle upon Tyne: Tel: 091-232 7575
Edinburgh: Tel: 031-443 8731
Cardiff: Tel: 0222 388588

These are also the offices to which notification of redundancies (if required) should be made (see Chapter 14).

Similar information is also available in the *Reference Book for Employers*, published by:

Croner Publications Ltd
Croner House
173 Kingston Road
New Malden
Surrey KT3 3SS
Tel: 081-942 8966

Appendix 2

Selecting consultants

Hiring consultants to help or advise in a turn-round situation may be necessary if you have neither the specialized skills nor the time available yourself. Choosing the *right* consultant is critical because:

- The cost will be high and the company has limited money resources.
- The problem is urgent, which means the right strategy and plans must be found *first* time.
- Bad advice could worsen the position and hasten the closure of the business.

There are five discrete steps to be considered:

- The scope of an assignment
- The short-list
- The initial discussions
- The proposal
- The final selection

THE SCOPE OF AN ASSIGNMENT

You may consider seeking consultancy help at the following levels:

- To help from beginning to end. This is the recommended option.

- To help prepare the strategy after you have gathered the necessary data. This option could reduce the cost, but many of the larger consultancy practices may not be prepared to accept data which they have not themselves collected or at least verified.
- To be a sounding board to which you can expose the strategy and plans you have already formulated, or to participate in the 'think tank' sessions described in Chapter 12.

THE SHORT-LIST

The first step is to make a short-list of possible consultants. A list of sources is to be found in Appendix 1. In addition to seeking possible consultants yourself, you may find some canvassing directly for business. The following are points worth bearing in mind:

- Successful consultancies generate the bulk of their business from client referrals. Seek a recommendation from any business colleagues who have had experience of using consultants successfully.
- Beware of any consultant who promises results without first having learned a great deal about your company. That is just sales talk.
- Ignore any who use 'hard selling' tactics. It means they need your business more than you need their help. Successful consultancies do not need to take this approach.
- Check whether or not the 'consultant' who visits you is in reality a self-employed salesperson. Reputable practices do not operate this way.

THE INITIAL DISCUSSIONS

Having formed a short-list, you should then meet each consultant on the short-list to discuss your problem and agree the possible scope of an assignment. Be prepared to spend a couple of hours with each of them. The following advice is pertinent at that stage:

- You should not pay for this meeting.
- Equally, you should not expect the consultant to give you free advice at this stage.
- Make it clear that your problem is specifically that of turning the company round.
- Give the consultant any background information he asks for.
- Indicate how far you have gone yourself in any fact-finding or analysis. Be prepared to table this, but do not at this stage hand over a copy of such information.
- Do not offer opinions as to what aspects of your business need improvement. If you do, you may receive a proposal to address only these areas, rather than one that addresses the wider picture.
- Do not volunteer an opinion as to what you think needs to be done. If you do, you may pay a lot of money just to have your own opinions repeated as recommendations in an imposing report.

THE PROPOSAL

What you should then expect from each consultant is some form of proposal. This should contain:

- A clear statement of the objective of a consultancy assignment, namely to provide you with a plan for turning your company round from losses into profit.
- The steps or methodology the consultant proposes using in tackling your problem.
- How long the project will take.
- How much it will cost.

An evaluation of these proposals will lead to your final choice of consultant. The yardsticks by which they can be assessed are the following:

- How clearly has the consultant understood the problem? Does it ring true as a statement of what your company's present position really is? If not, then you are probably wasting your time reading any further.

- Does the proposed methodology include the fundamental steps and methods outlined in this book? Make sure that the proposals are not too narrowly biased towards purely financial aspects of the business. To be relevant this project must include a great deal of study of your market-place and your position in that market.

THE FINAL SELECTION

In deciding which consultant to engage you must take the following factors into account:

- Whether or not the proposal satisfied the questions just asked of it.
- Your own judgement of whether or not the consultant seems capable of doing the job.
- Has the consultant a proven track record? The proof will be if he or she has been in an executive position and has actually turned a company round from loss to profit, or if he or she, as a consultant, has guided a client through a comparable turn round.
- Do the references bear that out? You need names and references, and you should pick up the telephone and check them out. No consultant who is worth your money will object to you talking to previous clients.
- Is the work going to be done by the consultant personally? If not, get the names of other members of the firm who will be involved. You have a right to meet them also and to check out their references.
- Will part of the work be subcontracted? If so, then you clearly need to assess the subcontractors as well. Two critical factors in this situation will be:
  - How much control the consultant will have over the sub-contractor. Is there a guarantee that the time-scale will be met?

– How the consultant will underwrite the quality of the subcontractor's work.

Your best guarantee of making a wise choice is knowing in advance precisely who is going to do the work and having proof that they have done a similar job successfully for a previous client.

Appendix 3

Setting up the accounting system

If the company does not have a computer-based accounting system, the following advice will assist in setting one up with the minimum of problems:

- Seek advice from your accountants or auditors regarding the choice of a suitable software package.
- Buy both hardware and software from a local dealer who will be able to provide support and maintenance on both items. Ask your auditors or a local colleague if they can recommend a dealer.
- Accept the dealer's advice on hardware, but be careful not to be persuaded to buy anything other than the least-cost option that will guarantee an efficient system.
- Seek the dealer's advice on what hardware options and how much fixed disk is needed. If the company is large enough to need access by more than one person to the system, you will need more than one PC and this will need some network software to link them together.
- Ensure that the dealer includes some provision for making the daily back-up as quick and painless as possible.
- If you are worried about the cost, talk to the bank manager. If you have not had proper accounts up to now, the bank manager may already have decided that this is the company's main weakness and will be supportive.
- Once the hardware and software are installed set the objective of getting management accounts from the new system by

no later than the month-end after next. This should not be
difficult, provided existing systems are capable of keeping up
to date with sales invoicing.

- Ask your auditors to build an appropriate nominal ledger
  coding system and give you the opening balances for the
  nominal ledger.
- Seek help from the auditors or the software supplier to
  support you in the initialization of the new system.
- Make sure the company's basic systems are streamlined
  enough to ensure that data entry of the following items are all
  up-to-date on a planned time schedule each month-end:
  – Sales and purchase invoices, credit notes and cash
  – Miscellaneous cash payments and receipts
- Seek advice from the auditors regarding the handling of the
  following month-end accounting tasks:
  – Calculation of accruals and pre-payments
  – Calculation of material cost of sales.

  In this context remember that it is always better to be
  approximately correct than to have no information at all, and
  any errors in estimated material costs will come out in the
  wash when a periodic stock check is carried out.
- At this stage do not get involved with any computer systems
  modules other than the ledgers, but do make certain that the
  sales and purchase ledgers automatically link to the nominal
  ledger.

Appendix 4

Stock checking

The company should have a stock checking and stock evaluation system which the auditors have agreed, and they should have been present at year-end stock checks to ensure that all is in order.

The following safeguards and checks should always be observed:

- Cut-off. Ensure that there is a rigid cut-off in paperwork. The valuation of stock will be meaningless unless you can account for the following:
  - Receipts not yet invoiced
  - Despatches not yet invoiced
  - Finished goods in stock but already invoiced
  - Sales invoices not posted to the ledger
  - Purchase invoices not posted to the ledger

  Do not assume that your accounts staff fully understand the implications of this; verify it for yourself.
- Stock check tickets. Insist on using stock check tickets. Count the stock check tickets out and count them back. Record who they were issued to and account for missing tickets.
- Nothing must move. Freeze the works and stores while the count is in progress; nothing must move until you say so, no matter how urgent it is to get production restarted.
- Completeness. Make sure every item is ticketed; if the counters have included more than one bundle, case or packet on one ticket, cross-check them against the ticket. Look in every nook and cranny and if anything is unticketed, challenge it.

- Do not accept excuses. Do *not* accept any of the following as reasons why an item has not been counted and recorded:
  - That item is fully written off.
  - That item was not counted last time.
  - That is customer's material.
  - That is scrap or damaged.
  - That is a customer return.

  Instead get your staff to record that information on the ticket and then sort it out later in your own office.
- Unidentified material. If anything is unidentified, make your quality manager identify it; this is the best person to do so.
- Only when you are absolutely certain that everything is counted and ticketed should you allow materials to start moving again.
- Materials outside the company. Identify any company materials being held by suppliers or subcontractors, and telex or fax them just before the stock check starts for a written confirmation of:
  - The stock they are holding.
  - Details of their latest despatch to you.
  - Details of their most recent receipt from you.

  This will not only confirm stock held outside the company; it will also help account for anything in transit at the time.
- Spot-checks. Carry out the normal spot checks on accuracy of counting and recording. The method used by the auditors will serve your purposes also.
- Pricing and evaluation. Invite your accounts and/or purchasing staff to price the tickets with you according to the company's standing conventions. You will learn a very great deal from this simple exercise.

Index